Champions!

Jim Leyritz's home run was the key hit of the Series.

Cecil Fielder was the Series hitting star.

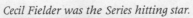

*David Cone led
the comeback.*

*A gritty Jimmy Key
came through
in game six.*

The final out; Charlie Hayes snared a foul pop.

Wade Boggs celebrated on horseback.

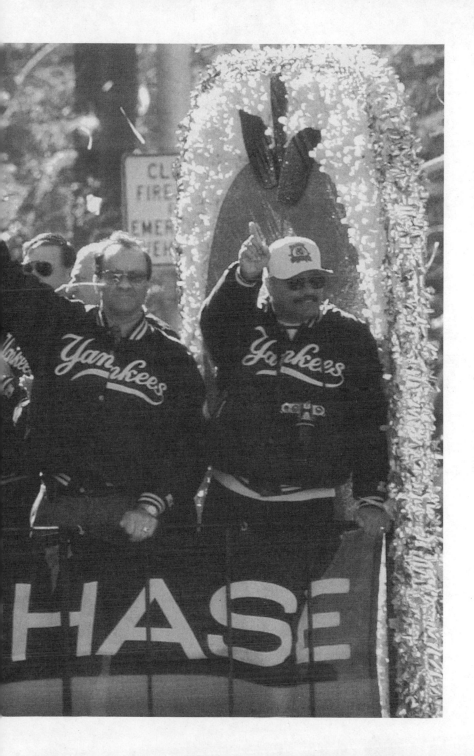

The Grand Celebration:
October 29, 1996,
Broadway, New York City

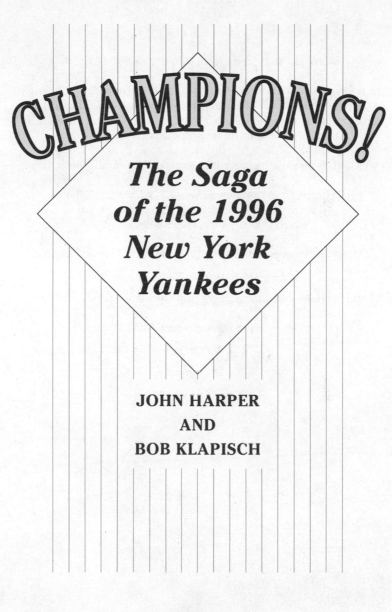

CHAMPIONS!

The Saga of the 1996 New York Yankees

JOHN HARPER
AND
BOB KLAPISCH

VILLARD
NEW YORK

Library of Congress Cataloging-in-Publication Data is available.

ISBN: 0-679-77840-3

Random House website address: http://www.randomhouse.com/

Printed in the United States of America on acid-free paper

2 4 6 8 9 7 5 3

FIRST EDITION

To Liz, Matt, and Chris,
who would have been rooting
for the Yankees anyway.
Just not as hard.
—JH

To Esther and Geoffrey Klapisch,
the home team
—BK

Preface

The foul pop-up had barely landed in Charlie Hayes's glove when a noise came out of Yankee Stadium that filled up the month of October. It is what miracles sound like. It is hugging and high-fiving and crazed shouting—grown men's substitutes for tears.

Still, in the middle of a sea of Yankees, there was Joe Torre, crying one last time in 1996. Crying, because a day after his brother Frank had successfully undergone a heart transplant, the Yankees had won their first World Series since 1978.

Champions. Rulers of the baseball world. The Yankees looked at one another in wild disbelief, still struggling to digest their own accomplishment: a 3–2 win over the Braves in game six that ended the most dramatic, most compelling Series in years. Down 0–2, the Yankees swept the last four games, and capped off their championship by beating the greatest pitcher of our generation, Greg Maddux.

"I look back at this World Series, and the last month, I think it was all supposed to happen," Torre said breathlessly. "You never like to leave anything to fate, but once we got here, it seemed like nothing could stop us."

Acknowledgments

We would like to thank David Rosenthal, Jennifer Webb, Leta Evanthes, Carole Lowenstein, Dan Rembert, Beth Pearson, and Amy Edelman at Villard for making this project a reality, and for dealing with all the eleventh-hour anxiety we caused them.

Contents

Preface   xiii
Introduction   xix

1   The Off Season   3
2   Spring Training   23
3   Orioles-Yankees, Act I   39
4   The Aneurysm   57
5   The Doctor Is In   69
6   The Straw That Stirs the Drink   85
7   The Sweeps   101
8   Low Tide Coming   115
9   The Crisis   131
10 The Resurgence   147
11 Home with the Rangers   163
12 Orioles-Yankees, the Final Act   175
13 A Classic Fall Classic   191

    1996 Season and Postseason Statistics   209

Introduction

It seems only fair.

Four years ago we wrote *The Worst Team Money Could Buy*, about a fairly miserable bunch of high-priced stars known as the 1992 New York Mets. Now along comes the best team money can buy, an admirable bunch of high-priced stars known as the 1996 New York Yankees.

We wanted a chance to tell a slightly more pleasant story. Indeed, a magical story.

It seems people everywhere have been moved by the tribulation and triumph that defined the Yankee season. Even in Hollywood. Dwight Gooden signed a deal to have a movie made of his life story, but, in truth, the entire march to the postseason played out like a scriptwriter's fantasy.

So many comebacks. So many heroes. So many remarkable moments. So many goose bumps.

Who'd have thought?

From the apparent chaos of last winter, when George Steinbrenner was being vilified everywhere for cutting loose Buck

Showalter and revamping his roster, came a ball club for the people, a team-oriented bunch who were the antithesis of the image of baseball players in the nineties.

From the distastefulness of the Showalter departure came the sweetest story in years: Brooklynite Joe Torre, amid his own personal tragedies, finally reaching the promised land of the World Series.

And from the snow that fell during the home opener to the rain that wouldn't go away in October, the Yankees brought the fall classic back to the Bronx for the first time since 1981.

It was an extraordinary run that seemed to have the feel of destiny: Gooden rising from the ashes of drug abuse and suspension to revive his career and throw a no-hitter only hours before his father would undergo open-heart surgery.

David Cone fooling everyone, even the doctors, by returning from the agony of aneurysm surgery to throw his own unofficial no-hitter and help save the Yankees from a second-half collapse.

Darryl Strawberry playing his way off the St. Paul Saints and back to the Bronx, electrifying the Yankee Stadium crowds by going deep again three times in one memorable night against the White Sox.

Jimmy Key coming back from shoulder surgery at age thirty-five and delivering the clutch performance of the year in game three against the Orioles.

Mariano Rivera turning into Superman.

The Yankees sweeping the mighty Cleveland Indians in a day-night doubleheader with Brian Boehringer and Mario Mendoza doing the honors on the mound.

The Yankees going 18-0 in Jacobs Field, Camden Yards, and Atlanta's Fulton County Stadium.

The postseason comebacks.

A twelve-year-old kid from New Jersey stealing a play-off win against the Orioles.

And there was Torre, after one brother died in June of a heart attack while watching a Yankees game and the other waited in a New York hospital for a heart transplant, crying openly as his ball club fulfilled his lifelong quest to reach the World Series.

It was a season from the Yankee archives, filled with the kind of drama and emotion that fans link with such legends as Babe Ruth, Lou Gehrig, Joe DiMaggio, and Mickey Mantle.

New stars emerged in 1996: Bernie Williams, Derek Jeter, Andy Pettitte, Mariano Rivera. A new Yankee era was born, and the best part was that they did it the right way: with hustle and heart and nary an ego problem in sight. They were fun to watch and easy to like.

What a difference four years make.

—JOHN HARPER
BOB KLAPISCH
October 1996

Champions!

Joe Torre

1

The Off Season

Two hours after Ken Griffey, Jr., slid across the plate, setting off the pandemonium that signaled the end of the Yankees' 1995 season, the Kingdome was finally quiet. Three thousand miles to the east, a city of passionate fans was in mourning. But in the Seattle press box a sense of dread was just building.

For the working stiffs whose job it is to report on the activities of a certain baseball team in the Bronx, the real season was just beginning.

It's not just the city of New York that never sleeps anymore. The information business is a Teletype machine on steroids these days; sports fans are bombarded with news and statistics and opinion and breakdown segments from their TVs, their radios, their on-line services, and yes, their morning papers too.

But as news is gulped down more instantaneously than ever, newspapers cling to the off season as their domain. The off season offers no highlights for TV; no managerial decisions for talk radio to dissect. Back-channel reporting, otherwise known as spending untold hours on the phone, is what uncovers the government secrets about who's being hired and fired, traded and signed, and for how many millions.

The stuff that sells newspapers; SportsCenter be damned.

Of course, to baseball writers just crossing the finish line of a marathon season, long days of working the phones and fretting over which reporter George Steinbrenner will favor with a callback has all the appeal of knee surgery.

And as everyone covering the Yankees knew at the time, with contracts expiring for the likes of Buck Showalter, Gene Michael, Don Mattingly, Wade Boggs, David Cone, Mike Stanley, and others, this off season would be no arthroscopic procedure. Reconstructive was more like it.

"It's gonna be brutal," someone moaned that night amid the tapping of fingers to keyboards. "Just brutal."

No one disagreed. But no one knew the truth either. Brutal turned out to be an apt description for the ensuing weeks on the Steinbrenner watch, but from a whirlwind of chaos and endless change would come the most enchanting season a baseball team could ever construct.

What George Steinbrenner didn't understand was how grateful Yankee fans were to manager Buck Showalter for restoring a sense of dignity to the pinstripes. What Steinbrenner did understand, however, is that in the end, fans believe in their own inalienable right to a championship team. They cheer for the uniforms, not the men who wear them.

And so formed the backdrop to the '96 season. More than a few times down the stretch in '95 Steinbrenner informed his high command he would draw a hard and fast line on his payroll for '96. He wouldn't spend a penny over $42 million,

George told Showalter and Gene Michael, and since the payroll stood at $46 million already, they had better be prepared to go bargain hunting in the winter.

But then he and Showalter parted company, and when fans howled in protest the Yankee budget grew like the national deficit.

"Tell 'em if they win they owe me a ring," Showalter joked to a friend one day as the Yankees closed in on the division title.

Joke or not, it was true. Showalter had reestablished a genuine sense of Yankee pride in the clubhouse. He and General Manager Gene Michael had made a conscious effort to weed out the Mel Halls and bring in a nucleus of unselfish players who created a team-oriented atmosphere, an atmosphere that made the transition to Joc Torre relatively easy. But more to the point, the backlash over Showalter's departure loosened the purse strings—suddenly no cost was too high for George Steinbrenner to win back the fans. Before all was said and done, the payroll would skyrocket into the $60 million range, all because of the owner's need to justify the manager's sudden departure.

Whatever the exact circumstances were surrounding the split, the fans put the blame squarely on Steinbrenner. Given his history with managers, it was inevitable.

Showalter, after all, was as popular with the fans as George was loathed for his years of meddling. Buck had earned a reputation as a guardian of the Yankee tradition and a man who put in longer office hours than a football coach—anything to give his team an edge.

When an inspired September run of 21–6 had earned the Yankees their first postseason berth since 1981, Steinbrenner himself got a little misty-eyed in the Toronto clubhouse the day of the clinching and declared Showalter's managing down the stretch to be pure brilliance.

"I don't know how Buck did it," Steinbrenner purred that day, "but everything he did worked. He managed like a genius."

By then Steinbrenner was getting his manager's name right. Showalter had been hired in 1992 by Gene Michael during Steinbrenner's two-year suspension from baseball—for paying off Howie Spira to dig up dirt on Dave Winfield. And often upon his return in 1993 Steinbrenner would refer to Buck as "Bucky," as in Dent.

It made Showalter mad as hell. He was sure George was doing it intentionally just to test him, but it wasn't Buck's style to confront The Boss, and eventually Steinbrenner dropped the "y."

Why not? Showalter was George's kind of manager: long hours and no lip.

Steinbrenner loved seeing Buck jot notes into the little notebook he carried with him, loved the fact that Buck arrived at the ballpark at dawn during spring training. Mostly he loved to win, and, if not for the players' strike, Showalter would have had the Yankees in position to win it all in 1994. They had the best record in the American League when the players walked out the door that August, not to return that season.

A year later Buck's boys overcame an awful August stretch to play like champs in September, in part because Showalter commanded enough respect to hold them together during a turbulent season. Buck's four-year tenure was already the longest continuous run of any manager in Steinbrenner's twenty-two years of ownership, and when the Yankees clinched the wild-card berth his return seemed to be a foregone conclusion.

George was in his glory that day. Oh, how he loved sitting in Blue Jays owner Pat Beeston's private box and celebrating right there along with Beeston—one of Steinbrenner's few allies among his fellow owners. He was a big shot again, back in the postseason.

In the clubhouse he walked from locker to locker, shaking hands with each of his players, telling everyone how proud he was of his manager and his ball club. The Boss can be such a charming fellow when the ball bounces his way. But losing turns him into a werewolf.

So it was that only a week after beaming in Toronto, he was howling at the moon in Seattle.

Steinbrenner didn't care if the Yankees and the Mariners had played an epic series that made America appreciate baseball again for the first time since the players' strike. A loss was a loss, goddammit, and blowing a 2–0 series lead to Lou Piniella was a heinous crime.

After game five Steinbrenner stood at the far end of the clubhouse, glaring toward the manager's office, where a drained Showalter had finished talking to the press and then put his head on his desk and cried. All around the room the anxiety and the emotion of the series came pouring out. Don Mattingly had tears in his eyes, as did David Cone. Hard as it was to lose, though, the players appreciated the intensity and the drama that made the series so memorable.

"If this is it, it's a hell of a way to go," Mattingly whispered that night, forecasting his semiretirement.

But for Steinbrenner there is no joy in competition itself, no gray between black and white. The Yankees had lost—someone had to pay. Most reporters wanted to ignore the owner that night. The series itself deserved their attention. But the sight of Steinbrenner inspires Pavlovian response from the press. To miss one of his diatribes is to ensure a lecture from your sports editor the next day. To miss what he might say after a season-ending loss is to ask for a new job.

"There are going to be changes here," Steinbrenner announced as reporters dutifully encircled him. "You can be sure of that."

So as the play-offs continued without the Yankees, no one was terribly surprised when Steinbrenner began dropping more hints that he might be interested in Davey Johnson, the ex–Met manager and lame-duck manager of the National League Central champion Reds.

But when the Orioles beckoned, Davey made it clear that the team he had played most of his career for was his priority. Steinbrenner didn't want to cough up the salary Tony LaRussa would command, and with no other hot names on the market, it began to look as if Showalter was a lock to come back.

In fact, it was Showalter who was in no hurry to sign a new deal when Steinbrenner finally agreed to meet with him at Yankee headquarters in Tampa, Florida, on October 20, nearly two weeks after game five with the Mariners.

Steinbrenner offered him a two-year deal to stay that would climb in the coming days to $1.05 million. Before signing anything, however, Showalter wanted to know who would be the new general manager replacing Stick Michael, a man he respected for his baseball knowledge and worked well with on personnel matters.

Michael, who had rebuilt a barren farm system, cultivating prospects who would prove vital to the '96 team, was rewarded for a job well done by being asked to take a pay cut— from $600,000 to $400,000. He stepped aside instead, taking a $150,000 scouting director's job in the organization that would end his stint of fifteen-hour days in the office and allow him to rediscover his golf game.

Now Showalter wanted to know with whom he'd be working. Problem was, nobody was lining up to be general manager for the Yankees. The legend of Hurricane George had spread far and wide. Several baseball executives declined to even consider the position when approached by Michael, who was conducting a search for his own replacement.

But Bob Watson, already the general manager of the Astros, leaped at the opportunity. What the heck, he'd beaten prostate cancer a year earlier, undergoing successful surgery; working for Steinbrenner couldn't be so tough. So on October 23, five hours after the Yankees first contacted him, Watson agreed to become Yankee general manager, signing a two-year deal worth $300,000 a year.

At that point, Steinbrenner seemed to fully expect Showalter to come back, indicating that he'd moved quickly to get a general manager, mostly at Showalter's request. But there were obstacles in the path to an agreement. Showalter wanted a three-year deal, and with word already leaking that teams such as the Tigers and A's wanted to talk to him about managing when his contract with the Yankees expired on October 31, he had leverage.

Steinbrenner wouldn't budge on his two-year offer, however. And he was insisting that Showalter fire three of his coaches, Rick Down, Brian Butterfield, and Glenn Sherlock. It was typical of Steinbrenner's need to dictate terms of employment to his employees. He'd picked on pitching coaches most often over the years when he felt a need to flex some muscle and send a message to a manager.

But in this case Steinbrenner was well aware that Down, Butterfield, and Sherlock formed Buck's inner circle, all of them career minor leaguers as players who were now enjoying life at the top. When Butterfield, whose late father, Jack, had worked for Steinbrenner as director of player development, heard of the rumblings, he drove to Tampa and confronted Steinbrenner in person.

For years Yankee employees who had the nerve found it was the only way to back down the bully. As ferocious as his bark could be, Steinbrenner didn't often bite when confronted. Countless times he had rescinded firings of executive personnel when someone demanded an explanation, and in this case he was quick to assure Butterfield that he had no problem with him. His job was safe.

Eventually, Steinbrenner agreed to retain Sherlock as well. But he wouldn't relent on Down, and the hitting instructor was too proud to give Steinbrenner the satisfaction of confronting him. He figured his record spoke for itself; since his arrival in 1993 the Yankees had become one of the most productive offensive teams in baseball, leading the league in batting average in '94 and '95. More significantly, his work seemed to have a clear impact on hitters such as Paul O'Neill, Wade Boggs, Mike Stanley, and Randy Velarde, all of whom either blossomed or rediscovered their stroke during those years. They loved to talk hitting with Down and appreciated that he was on call at any time for extra batting practice.

But Steinbrenner was determined to wield his power in some way. He wanted Down out, telling Showalter it was a personal issue based on a comment that Down had allegedly made at some point in the season to Arthur Richman, the seventy-year-old media relations adviser who was one of the owner's confidants. Richman would only drop hints that Down had offended him in some way. Down, meanwhile, insisted he knew nothing about it. There had always been tension between Richman and the Showalter staff, however, because Richman was viewed as a spy of sorts for Steinbrenner. And there had been a moment in Seattle, according to a person who witnessed it, when Richman was bemoaning the Yankees' fate in Showalter's office after the Mariners had come back to tie the series 2–2, and Down essentially told him to take a hike.

In any case, Showalter defended Down fiercely to Steinbrenner and insisted he wouldn't sign a new deal if his hitting coach was going to be whacked.

As it was, Showalter had been preparing himself to move on. He knew that Steinbrenner's bumping of Michael was a sign the owner wanted to take more control again in the day-to-day baseball operations, and he figured that meant misery for him. Showalter was far more shrewd and calculating than his public image belied; his attention to detail and his encyclopedic awareness of all those around him was part of what made him such a good manager. If he was going to stay, he wanted it to be worth his while.

Still, the Yankees meant the world to him. It was the only organization he'd ever known, first as a minor-league outfielder who didn't hit enough to advance to the big leagues with Double A teammate Don Mattingly and then as a manager who had worked his way to the top, one step at a time.

He desperately wanted to be the manager who took the Yankees back to the World Series for the first time since 1981.

"It would mean a lot to me, and it would make all the aggravation worthwhile," he said during a quiet moment in his office in 1993.

So maybe, in the end, Showalter miscalculated. When he phoned Steinbrenner that afternoon to say he was turning down the two-year offer, he gave the owner an opening to make a change that George wouldn't have to call a firing. The Boss hung up the phone and immediately ordered Richman to write a news release saying that Showalter had resigned, and within a couple of hours it had been faxed to PR director Rob Butcher and distributed in Cleveland, where everyone but the New York media was having an enjoyable time covering the World Series.

Showalter seemed genuinely shocked that night as he took calls from reporters. He said Steinbrenner had given him no indication that their phone call had been final. He said he had heard of his so-called resignation when his wife phoned him in his car after hearing it on the radio.

But what was done was done. The very next day Steinbrenner and his lieutenants were leaking word that Joe Torre was the likely successor. Again Richman played a role. A longtime friend of Torre, Richman had been touting the Brooklyn product for years to Steinbrenner and told him Torre's calm, assured style would make him the perfect successor. Perhaps even more significantly, Gene Michael recommended Torre as well. He'd always thought highly of him, and, after interviewing him for the GM job only a week earlier, Michael felt Torre would be a good choice as well. He recommended him to Steinbrenner as an astute baseball man whose lousy managerial record was merely the result of too many bad teams in previous stints with the Mets, Braves, and Cardinals—the team that had fired him during the '95 season.

A swift decision was made, and a week later Torre was introduced at a press conference in New York. The Showalter era was officially over. But it might have been reopened before Torre ever put on the Yankee uniform, thanks to what was perhaps Steinbrenner's most bizarre act of all last winter.

When the hiring of Torre was panned by the press (in particular Mike Lupica of the *Daily News*) as grasping for a retread manager with a losing record, it added to the public furor over the Showalter affair. Steinbrenner was more and more troubled by the reaction, to the point where a few weeks later he showed up unannounced at Showalter's house in Pensacola, Florida. He stunned Showalter by offering him a chance to come back, preferably in the form of an agreement to replace Torre in a year or two, as George had done once with Billy Martin after a similarly unpopular firing. But if it was the only way to lure him back, Steinbrenner was willing to rename Showalter as manager immediately and reassign Torre to another position in the organization. By that time Buck was close to signing with the Arizona Diamondbacks, and he couldn't imagine humiliating Torre that way. The Yankee blood in him made it tempting, but Showalter said no thanks. Steinbrenner walked away unhappy that day. He must have wondered if New York would ever forgive him for hiring Joe Torre.

The weeks following the Torre press conference produced a dizzying succession of personnel moves. The off-season mania that had started with the Buck and George showdown only escalated in November and December. It was a rare day when football or basketball or hockey, the sports actually being played, took the back page of the tabloids away from the Yankees, as a picture of chaos emerged from Yankee headquarters in Tampa.

First there was the suspense surrounding the immediate future of Don Mattingly, then tributes for the Yankee captain when he told Steinbrenner to go ahead without him in '96.

There was the outrage over the dumping of Mike Stanley for Joe Girardi. And more fury when Randy Velarde signed with the California Angels.

There was the silence from the Yankees as Jack McDowell signed with the Cleveland Indians.

There was the confusion surrounding the on-again, off-again trade for Tino Martinez. Yankee indecision turned it into an uproarious affair, played out in the papers for a solid week before Steinbrenner finally agreed to pull the trigger and send Russ Davis and Sterling Hitchcock to Seattle for Martinez and Jeff Nelson.

Through it all, there was also the matter of David Cone, the best pitcher in the free-agent market and a lightning rod for the Yankees-Orioles rivalry that would come to define the '96 season.

After failing to deliver a win in game five against the Mariners, Cone had fought depression. For three weeks he rarely so much as left his apartment on Manhattan's East Side, as he dealt with the loss and began to sort out in his mind the decision that lay in front of him.

As he began to surface from his hibernation, he was heartened by what he called "unbelievable support" from New Yorkers he encountered in restaurants and walking around the city. People would shake his hand and urge him to re-sign with the Yankees, even thanking him for his heroic 145-pitch effort in game five.

New York had long felt like home for Cone, going back to his days with the Mets. When he played in Toronto and Kansas City, he kept his New York apartment, spending much of the winter in Manhattan. He'd always found the human climate in New York to be far warmer than its reputation, and he liked having a few dozen different restaurants within walking distance as well.

But he was in no hurry to make a decision now that he was a free agent again. Perhaps more than anyone, he was concerned about the personnel changes he was reading about in the newspapers every day.

So when the Cleveland Indians called to say they wanted him badly, but only if he were willing to make a quick decision, Cone passed and the Tribe signed McDowell.

It was early December before Cone got serious about a decision. By then he had lunched with Torre and Watson and come away tremendously impressed.

"I'd heard nothing but good things from guys who had played for Torre," Cone would say. "And I could see why. He just had a calm, assured manner about him. We had a great talk, and that turned out to be a big factor."

At the same time, he felt a tug to the south. As an activist in the Players Association, Cone felt a debt of gratitude toward Peter Angelos over the Orioles' owner's refusal to go along with the replacement-player scam during the labor strike. And he had great respect for the Orioles' new general manager, Pat Gillick, and new manager, Davey Johnson. Gillick had made the trade as Toronto Blue Jays general manager in 1992 to acquire Cone from the Mets and enable him to win a world championship, and Johnson had managed him during the good times as a Met.

For weeks Cone tried to sort out the pros and cons, knowing the money was likely to be about even, knowing that his decision could shift the balance of power in the American League East. Finally, in mid-December both teams were applying pressure for an answer.

Steinbrenner invited Cone and his agent, Steve Fehr, to Tampa. Together with Bob Watson they toured the Yankees' new spring-training facility, then settled down in Steinbrenner's office. The Boss launched into a speech about Yankee tradition. He said that with Mattingly gone, he viewed Cone as the new Mr. Yankee, the pinstriped leader.

Then Steinbrenner suggested that Watson and Fehr adjourn to a separate room to crunch numbers while he and Cone continued to talk. Watson laid out the offer that essentially would be the one Cone would accept, three years for $18 million, plus two option years that could be triggered automatically if Cone stayed healthy. Should the option years not kick in, the Yankees could buy them out for $1.5 million, making the deal worth a guaranteed $19.5 million.

It was exactly what Cone was hoping to hear. He told Steinbrenner he needed the weekend to talk it over with his wife, Lynn, but he flew home thinking that the deal was all but done. But then a day later Watson called Fehr to tell him the Yankees were changing their offer, taking one of the option years out of the deal and lowering the buyout by $500,000. Steinbrenner had reduced the offer to more closely match the deal Jack McDowell had received from the Indians, though Watson gave Fehr no explanation for the changes.

Cone was furious upon hearing the news and immediately had Fehr call the Orioles.

"To me it was a challenge to go and talk to Baltimore," Cone would say months later. "What that did was send me to talk to the Orioles for the first time in a formal way. To that point no formal offers had been exchanged."

Now Cone had a reason not to sign with the Yankees. Fehr called Gillick and made a proposal approaching the numbers in the original Yankee offer.

"We told them that if they accepted the offer," Cone later recalled, "I would be an Oriole. We called it an exclusive right to sign me. I told them I wasn't going to take their offer back to the Yankees. I was theirs if they wanted me."

The numbers were high for the Orioles, who had made Roberto Alomar their top priority in the free-agent market and knew they needed a front-line bull-pen closer as well. And after a couple of rounds of counteroffers, they were close enough early in the day on Wednesday, December 20, that Cone said the Orioles "were making plans to call a press conference."

But the Orioles wanted Cone to defer as much as $5 million of the three-year, $18 million offer, as Alomar wound up agreeing to do. Cone wasn't willing, and the two sides haggled over deferred money as Wednesday dragged on.

By then Fehr was negotiating directly with Angelos. The Orioles' owner would later recall that at some point he told Fehr he'd confer with his accountants and get back to him on the deferred money. That pause turned out to be critical.

While Cone was waiting for an answer, Steinbrenner called from a pay phone outside a Tampa hospital, where he was visiting a friend. He'd caught wind that Cone was close to signing with the Orioles and was calling to say the lowering of the offer was all a mistake. In other words, he blamed it on Watson.

"He said it was a miscommunication between him and Watson," Cone later recalled. "He said everything was back on the table, and he said, 'Look, I'm not signing you to trade you. I want you to be a Yankee the rest of your career. If you want a no-trade clause you've got it.' "

For Cone, tired of being treated as a hired gun during pennant races, the no-trade clause was critical. Suddenly, the Yankees were the front-runners again. But the Orioles could have had him.

"What I should have said was 'Hold the line,' " Angelos would say months later, referring to his call to Fehr. "That's where we were. I would have given Cone two no-trade clauses."

Too late. Cone was beginning to think like a Yankee again.

At that moment the phone rang again. To Cone's complete surprise, it was John Franco, his ex–Met teammate, who had been following the story as well as the much-chronicled Yankee chaos. Franco knew Cone wanted to stay in New York and figured the Mets, with their heralded young pitching, might tempt him.

Cone was immediately intrigued, in part because at this point his brain was fried and he was looking for an answer.

"I told Johnny I was feeling kind of lost," Cone recalled. "I had a connection to New York, but I also had a lot of respect for Angelos and Gillick, and negotiations were a little crazy right now. He started feeling me out about coming back to the Mets, and I said, 'Wouldn't that be wild?'

"But I told him we had called the Mets early on and Joe McIlvaine never even returned my phone call. When I called them, things were crazy with the Yankees—I knew the Mets had some young talent, and I figured I ought to take a closer look, especially if the Yankees were going to be in a turnover phase. When they didn't call back, I forgot about it."

But now Franco, Mets owner Fred Wilpon's favorite player, was telling Cone to sit tight. Franco immediately called Mets PR director Jay Horwitz and told him to get General Manager Joe McIlvaine on the phone with Cone right away.

"He's really up in the air," Franco told Horwitz. "We might be able to get him."

Five minutes later McIlvaine was on the phone to Cone, telling him he'd like to set up a meeting if Cone was serious about the Mets.

At 8 A.M. the next day, McIlvaine knocked on Cone's East Side apartment door. No agent, no club lawyer. It was McIlvaine and Cone, two men forever linked in Met history. McIlvaine had built a reputation in the eighties as a sharp operator, in no small part because he'd made the trade of the decade in 1987, sending backup catcher Ed Hearn and a couple of no-name minor leaguers to the Kansas City Royals for Cone, then an unproven young talent on a team well stocked with pitching at the time.

Together now they reminisced briefly about the deal, about the old days with the Mets. McIlvaine was the San Diego Padres' general manager by the time Cone was traded to Toronto in 1992. But as McIlvaine spoke it became clear to Cone that he had some concerns about the pitcher's reputation as a media favorite. Management had long suspected that Cone was one of the anonymous sources feeding writers with information about and criticism of the club when the Mets began to stumble in the nineties. But in truth it was Cone's candor and stand-up behavior that made him such a saint in the eyes of the press corps.

Having once considered becoming a sportswriter for a living before his fastball took him other places, Cone wasn't much for cover-ups. When Buddy Harrelson asked him to lie to the press about their near fight in the dugout in 1991, which was caught on the TV cameras, Cone refused and told the media exactly what had happened, infuriating the manager.

Now McIlvaine was subtly lecturing Cone about the need for discretion should he actually come back, the need for Cone to set the right kind of example for the Mets' young players.

"He wanted to know what kind of leader I'd be," Cone recalled. "He wanted to look me in the eye and get his own feel for it."

Of course, Cone wasn't quite the free spirit he had been as a young Met. His role as a spokesman for the Players Association during the strike in 1994 seemed to change him forever. He was still very much a stand-up guy, but he was more cautious, more calculating in his dealings with the media.

Finally, McIlvaine was sufficiently satisfied to tell Cone he would make him an offer that afternoon. A couple of hours later he returned with David Howard, the club's vice president who handled contract negotiations. Together they laid out a three-year offer worth $15 million that included a limited no-trade clause.

As Cone saw it, the offer was nice enough, but it didn't compare with Steinbrenner's. So the choice was this: he could have New York and relative sanity for $15 million, or he could have the Bronx Zoo for $19.5 million.

For Cone there really was no choice. His dealings with the Players Association had made him more the businessman than ever, and yet he still had a wild side in him that made him a perfect fit in George Steinbrenner's kingdom.

"Personality-wise, this is where I belong," he would tell *The New York Times* after he signed. "I belong on the Yankees.

Maybe I'm a little rough around the edges and a little brash. On the other hand, I'm not afraid to speak my mind. Maybe this is the spot for me. Maybe I do belong in the zoo."

In the end, it wasn't sanity he was seeking. The Orioles had blown the chance to nail him when he was ticked at Steinbrenner for lowering his offer. Otherwise, only an outrageous deal, the kind he had signed with Kansas City three years earlier when then owner Ewing Kauffman gave him $9 million of an $18 million deal up front as a signing bonus, would have driven Cone to another ball club.

So finally, late in the afternoon on that Thursday, he said no thanks to the Mets and the Orioles and yes to George. At last, Yankee fans could exhale.

But the war with the Orioles was just beginning. The Birds signed Alomar and B. J. Surhoff the same day Cone signed with the Yankees, four days before Christmas. There would be no truce over the holidays either. Even as Cone and Alomar were signing, Cincinnati Reds general manager Jim Bowden was trying to get the general managers of each club on the phone. Ordered to slash his payroll, Bowden was peddling David Wells, a quality left-hander whom both the O's and Yankees had tried to acquire the previous summer.

Bowden, once fired as an assistant general manager with the Yankees, asked for Mariano Rivera and Ruben Rivera. Watson said forget it. So Bowden dealt Wells to the Orioles for a couple of lesser prospects, outfielders Curtis Goodwin and Trovin Valdez.

The deal was completed the day after Christmas. Steinbrenner felt compelled to match. Three days later, he was in his element as ringmaster of his own little circus in Tampa. By now New York had become little more than a substation for winter operations; all the action was in George's hometown.

In one room of the Yankee complex, Tim Raines was being introduced at a press conference. In another sat Kenny Rogers, and in still another was Chuck Finley, both being courted by the Yankees. Steinbrenner, meanwhile, zigzagged from room to room, welcoming Raines while conducting simultaneous negotiations with two of the best left-handers in baseball. Associates would say The Boss was nothing short of giddy as he reveled in the wheeling and dealing.

"It was George's favorite day of the whole winter," a person who was in the complex that day would say. "He was in his glory."

The Yankees could have had Finley for $14 million over three years, but at age thirty-one Rogers was two years younger, coming off a seventeen-win season. Never mind that everyone who knew Rogers in Texas was sure that New York was a bad fit for a quiet, small-town kid from rural Florida; on paper he was the best pitcher, so while Torre favored Finley, Steinbrenner gave Rogers $20 million over four years to become a Yankee.

People in the baseball world shook their heads. This was Steinbrenner at his most outlandish, desperately throwing money at players for his rotisserie team. But the same people had to admit that given the chance they would have signed Rogers themselves. The contract may have been unwarranted, the personality fit was a gamble, but what did George care?

In the blink of an eye, it seemed, Steinbrenner had put the talk of chaos to rest. By signing Cone and Rogers the Yankees were instantly transformed from a disorganized mess to a legitimate contender again. Still, some fan and media disenchantment over the changes lingered in New York. Skepticism too. Payroll aside, the Showalter Yankees had earned a blue-collar, all-for-one-and-one-for-all image that fans associated with the club's storied tradition.

Who knew what the new regime of Torre and Watson—National League carpetbaggers to many a die-hard Yankee fan—would bring? Mattingly, regarded as the link to Yankee legends by the masses, was gone, and with him all of his class. Same for Stanley and Velarde, both quiet, tough guys.

Money couldn't buy a championship; the Yankees and Mets had each proven the point at one time or another over the last fifteen years. Why would this team be any different?

2

Spring Training

The manager leaned back in his chair, took a long pull on his cigar, and laughed. It was the easy, anxiety-free laugh of a man who didn't seem to care that his salary checks were being signed by George Steinbrenner or that so many talented men before him had met the same fate.

"What happens if I get fired?" Torre said, repeating the question. "If that's the worst thing that can happen to me, then all I can say is that I'm ready for it. It's happened to me before. It's nothing worse than what I've already lived through."

With that, Torre took another hit on that ever-present cigar. Everything about the manager's office had a different feel to it than a year before. Even the most casual observer could see that Torre, as an outsider to the Yankee community, was looser than Showalter and certainly less obsessed with Steinbrenner.

Kenny Rogers

Maybe it was because Torre was sixteen years older than Showalter or that, at the age of fifty-five, he had just had his first child with his wife of nine years, Alice. Or maybe it was as Torre said, that after having been fired three times already in his career—by the Mets, the Braves, and the Cardinals—there was no way for Steinbrenner to truly wound him.

The real question, of course, was whether Steinbrenner would torture Torre the same way he'd overpowered Showalter—with the daily phone calls, the second guessing, and, even in the days of silence, that unrelenting pressure that, somehow, made Showalter feel as if his job were in the balance every single day of the season.

Buck's response to The Boss's meddling had been to lose himself in preparation. There were so many nights when he'd stay up late, reviewing tapes of games, especially after losses, wondering if there was something he could have done—some strategy the Yankees could have employed—that would have changed the result. That was part of Showalter's perfectionist nature. But another reason Buck worked so hard—why he would sleep so little, show up at the park so early, drown himself in scouting reports—was that he always wanted to have an answer ready when Steinbrenner picked up the phone and demanded an explanation.

In a sense, Buck became a tragic hero, someone who always lived with the expectation of his own downfall. He was a good man and an extraordinarily well-rounded and well-respected baseball executive. But after three years of managing the Yankees, something had been squeezed out of Buck. There didn't seem to be any real pleasure in his team's winning; he was too busy preparing his defense for the next crisis with George.

In fact, when the Yankees lost game five of the division series to the Mariners, there was no escaping the pathos of the scene in the manager's office: there was Buck, head pressed into his desk, shoulders shaking, his body language full of defeat. Showalter knew the Yankees' dream of making it to the World Series was over, and, with it, probably his own job too.

He was right, of course: losing to Lou Piniella incurred a debt one could never repay Steinbrenner.

So here was Torre, whose managerial record was less than distinguished. New Yorkers knew him as the former-Brooklynite-turned-star who won the Most Valuable Player Award in 1971 and was later manager of the hapless Mets. Under Torre the Mets finished last three years in a row and never better than fourth until his dismissal after the 1981 season.

Torre enjoyed his only success as part of the Braves' brief resurrection in the early eighties, winning a division in his first year in Atlanta. Even though Torre's Braves won their first thirteen games, the summer of '82 ended on a sour note, as Atlanta nearly squandered its nine-game lead to the Dodgers. The race in the West went down to the last day of the regular season, as the Braves clung to a one-game lead. Somehow, the Braves blew a chance to close out the race by themselves, losing to the Padres, but thanks to Joe Morgan's three-run homer off Dodger reliever Terry Forster, Los Angeles lost to the Giants, 5–3, and the Braves headed to the play-offs for the first time since getting swept by the Mets in 1969.

Torre ended up getting swept too, in three straight games to the Cardinals, and, two years later, he was swept away by Ted Turner. From there, Torre landed in St. Louis, inheriting the downside of the Whitey Herzog era. And although he did a respectable job for a franchise that was on an austerity kick, Torre never approached the godlike status that was bestowed upon the White Rat.

Torre was eventually fired in 1995, without ever having won more than eighty-seven games. By the end he'd grown disenchanted with the growing arrogance of major-league players and was particularly turned off by the ugly politics of the strike.

In fact, when the Cardinal players started to question Torre's loyalty for managing replacement players—and when he saw the Players Association threatening to cut off his coaches' licensing money because of their involvement with the scabs—Torre had finally cut the emotional cord with managing. He had worked as a broadcaster for the California Angels between previous managing stints, and he was ready to return to that life.

"It's easy, much, much easier than managing," Torre said. "At least as a broadcaster you knew that when you came home at night, you were able to leave the game at the ballpark. It didn't eat you up twenty-four hours a day the way managing would."

Indeed, Torre was perfect for the broadcast booth: intelligent, well spoken, and, above all, fair-minded. Yet there he sat in the manager's office in late February, ready to pick up where Showalter had failed. Why? It hardly seemed worth it, even at $500,000, which was less than Torre had been earning as a broadcaster.

Why, when Torre knew he'd be the fodder for the second guessers on WFAN and headline writers at the *Post* and *Daily News*? Why, when, sooner or later, Torre would be fired just like all the rest?

To all these questions, Torre's dark, dark eyes would brighten. Why? "Because I thought it was a perfect chance for me to get to the World Series. Maybe my last chance," Torre said. "All the stories that I'd heard about George . . . at least I knew that he wanted to win. With all my years with the Mets and the Cardinals, I'd never worked for an owner that was so committed to winning and putting the best possible players on the field."

It sure looked that way, especially as Torre gazed into the clubhouse and saw Tino Martinez taking over for Don Mattingly, David Cone re-signed at $6 million per, Kenny Rogers replacing Jack McDowell, Mariano Duncan replacing Randy Velarde. Except for the loss of Mike Stanley, who was allowed to leave as a free agent without so much as a phone call from General Manager Bob Watson, the 1996 Yankees seemed to be improved over the '95 version.

In fact, Torre put himself directly on the spot in the very first days of camp, telling the press corps, "I expect us to go to the World Series. I really like our chances." The eight beat reporters who cover the Yankees—from the *Post*, the *Daily News*, the *Times*, *Newsday*, Gannett/Westchester-Rockland, the *Hartford Courant*, the Newark *Star-Ledger*, and the Bergen *Record*—paused a moment in stunned silence.

Never once, in Showalter's three years, had the manager ever uttered so blatant a prediction. The World Series? That was handing Steinbrenner the noose with which Torre could hang himself. But that turned out to be just another example of how different the Torre regime would be from Showalter's and, ultimately, why he was able to survive in The Boss's fiefdom.

Truth was, Torre didn't really need the job and was immune to the embarrassment and angst of getting fired. And, finally, what really would save Torre's sanity was a promise exacted from Steinbrenner by Watson, who, in accepting the job as Gene Michael's replacement, made just one request of Steinbrenner. Watson wanted to know for sure that The Boss wouldn't abuse his manager on the telephone. Steinbrenner said yes, and so began the Joe Torre administration, which had only one destination on its itinerary: October.

The Yankees' Tampa spring-training complex is a microcosm of the franchise that built it: massive, corporate, intimidating.

Unlike most spring-training fields, which offer an intimate setting for tourists and senior citizens, the Yankees' Legends Field is . . . well, a stadium, holding nearly ten thousand fans and costing nearly $30 million to construct. It was all part of Tampa's plan to lure the Yankees away from Fort Lauderdale, and the city's elders sure knew how to appeal to Steinbrenner, with the absolute biggest spring-training facility of them all.

If Steinbrenner couldn't have Camden Yards or Jacobs Field, if his Yankees had to be stuck in the South Bronx through the year 2002, then at least he could impress the baseball community with his Florida estate, located right in the heart of Tampa on Dale Mabry Highway. It was all there too: the club's minor-league facility, corporate offices, three practice fields, four underground batting cages, a complete weight room that would match the best of Gold's Gym, and, inside the clubhouse, the best team Steinbrenner could have possibly purchased.

True, he didn't have Robby Alomar, having lost the bidding war to Peter Angelos. But the Yankees still had Tino Martinez, one of the Mariners who was so instrumental in ending Showalter's reign. Tino was a shy, sometimes even nervous Tampa native who had one of the sweetest swings in the American League. Just about everyone in the league said Martinez would have few problems in New York—especially with that 314-foot right-field wall—as long as he got off to a good start.

"He can be a little sluggish in April," Lou Piniella said. "But if the fans are patient with him, they'll be very pleased. That young man can hit." The Mariners would have loved to have kept Tino, but General Manager Woody Woodward was ordered to trim the payroll, and with Ken Griffey consuming $7.5 million all by himself in 1996—and Griffey, Randy Johnson, and Jay Buhner costing the team more than $18 million—there was no choice but to move Martinez to a big market.

Martinez found out in a hurry what it means to hold a negotiating edge over Steinbrenner, who was desperate to fill the Don Mattingly void. Between Mattingly and Showalter—not to mention Gene Michael, Mike Stanley, and Randy Velarde—the Yankees were undergoing a massive face-lift, even by their own standards of instability.

That's why Steinbrenner wanted Martinez signed for five full years—to give the position some continuity. But Martinez and his agent, Jim Krivacs, who also represented Mattingly, were shocked to discover just how high Steinbrenner's ceiling really was.

When The Boss offered $20 million for five years, both Krivacs and Martinez swallowed hard. At $4 million per, the Yankees had exceeded Martinez's wildest expectations, since he was only going to ask for $3 million. So the first baseman and his agent excused themselves from the room and privately high-fived each other in delirium. They took a few minutes to compose themselves, then returned to shake hands.

As it turned out, signing a five-year pact was the easy part for Martinez. What lay ahead was living in Mattingly's shadow. Over and over, Martinez would repeat the same answer to reporters, who naturally wondered what it was like to replace a legend.

"I'm not replacing him. I didn't push him out," Martinez said, almost pleading. "I just happen to be the next guy playing first base for the Yankees. Donnie is a great player, a great guy. But he made this decision. I didn't get traded for him, I didn't take his job. He retired."

Joe Girardi had the same problems dealing with questions about Mike Stanley, who just happened to be one of the toughest, most decent Yankee players of the early nineties. It sure didn't help Girardi that Stanley was almost booted out of the Bronx by the Yankee regime.

But it was clear from the beginning that Watson and Torre were ready to implement a National League philosophy. And after he and Torre watched tapes of Stanley behind the plate, Watson said, "We just didn't feel he was as strong defensively as Girardi."

That was probably true, although, as it turned out, Girardi threw out just 21 of 103 base stealers in the regular season. Stanley ended up signing with the Red Sox as a free agent and hit twenty-four home runs before his season was cut short by a herniated disc in his neck.

Even as far away as Fort Myers, almost two hours from Tampa, Stanley had heard that Girardi was having a turbulent adjustment to New York. Not because of the players, of course, but the fans. In fact, Girardi, who had yet to play an inning in the Bronx, was booed by fans at the YankeeFest in Manhattan, a three-day, midwinter affair held at the New York Coliseum, where the public gets a chance to meet the players in person in an informal setting away from the ballpark.

It was hardly a warm reception, but Girardi seemed to understand the public's loyalty to Stanley. And so did Stanley, who sent Girardi a telegram from the Sox training facility. "Good luck in the coming year," said the former Yankee catcher. The message was simple, direct, and effective. Girardi said, "It was a classy thing to do. It showed me what kind of human being Mike is."

Eventually, Girardi would be entrusted with the Yankees' most precious commodity—their pitching. For all the Yankees' remaking, it was still the starting rotation that would decide whether the Orioles could be tamed.

In fact, all you had to do was walk into the clubhouse and make an immediate left turn. There they were, their lockers all in a row: Cone, Dwight Gooden, Kenny Rogers, Andy Pettitte, Melido Perez, and John Wetteland. For some reason,

Jimmy Key, who was rehabbing from a torn rotator cuff, was placed at the back of the clubhouse with reliever Paul Gibson. Maybe that's because Key still considered himself a separate entity from the starters, still unsure whether he'd be healthy enough to come north with the Yankees in April.

Key was the coolest of the cool—a man's man who, in Wetteland's words, "has the respect of everyone in this clubhouse—not just because of the way he pitches, but how he conducts himself. That's why it was so shocking last year when we found out Jimmy got hurt. It was like, 'Wow, how could anyone that good get hurt?' It was the same thing when I was with the Dodgers. No one could believe it when Orel [Hershiser] blew out his rotator cuff."

The uncertainty of Key's shoulder and the defection of Jack McDowell to the Indians were two reasons Steinbrenner went after Kenny Rogers, the soft-spoken left-hander who'd won seventeen games with the Rangers in 1995. No one disputed Rogers's ability: with his funky, short-arm delivery and huge, looping curveball, Rogers could be murder on left-handed hitters. His change-up could be just as effective against righties too, thanks to a fadeaway, two-seam fastball that hitters had to chase even at eighty-two miles per hour.

Rogers was a prize all right—quite a catch for the Yankees, thanks to David Cone's telephone recruiting work. But there was an overriding question about Rogers, and it had nothing to do with his arm. What Rogers's former employers wanted to know was whether he could handle the scrutiny of being a $5-million-a-year player in New York.

It wasn't an unfair question, since there had been dozens of players who were crushed by the tabloids, the callers on WFAN, and the raging impatience of the fans at Yankee Stadium itself. As Reggie Jackson used to say, "There's a difference between a good player and a good player in New York."

The classic example is Ed Whitson, who was so thoroughly intimidated by the Yankee reality in 1985 that he was no longer allowed to pitch in the Bronx. Ever since, every free agent who comes to New York has to answer a singular litmus test: Is he another Ed Whitson?

The Rangers privately wondered why Rogers, a Tampa native who is even more shy than Martinez, would even consider the Yankees. "Is it really the money?" one Rangers executive asked during the winter. "Kenny's a nice guy, but he doesn't know what he's getting himself into."

Part of the lure was, naturally, cash. The Yankees offered Rogers $20 million for four years, with the chance to earn another $5 million in the year 2000 if he pitched a mere two hundred innings in the previous summer. The Rangers' four-year offer was almost as seductive—$18 million—but what it really lacked, at least according to Rogers, was the promise of a division winner.

"I'd never gotten close before. I'd never been on a winner," Rogers said. "I thought this was going to be my chance, maybe the best one I was going to get."

Rogers was wrong, of course, since the Rangers eventually won the Western Division and made it to the postseason for the first time in the franchise's thirty-six-year history. But Rogers had other worries in February, starting with a batting-practice line drive that came screaming off Tony Fernandez's bat. Normally, a pitcher uses a protective screen to shield himself from such hazards, but on this day, Rogers recalled, "I just moved it aside because it was bothering my follow-through."

He paid dearly for that, as the ball hit him atop the shoulder, right at the point of the shoulder blade. He had instinctively tried to turn away from the line drive but, in doing so, only exposed his shoulder more completely. For a moment, all activity stopped at Legends Field, the impact was so loud. Joe

Torre and pitching coach Mel Stottlemyre immediately rushed to the mound, where Rogers kept repeating, over and over, that he was fine. But after two warm-up tosses, it was obvious that something was quite wrong.

Rogers was escorted off the field, and, as he crossed the first-base foul line, Fernandez looked over and said, "Sorry, man." Rogers smiled sheepishly and said, "Don't worry about it. Nothing you could do." Indeed, Rogers was more embarrassed than anything. For two weeks, he'd tried so hard just to blend in with the rest of the Yankees, wanting to be just another millionaire pitcher, looking for a way to prove his critics in Texas wrong.

Maybe that's why Rogers spent only three days on the sidelines and never let his shoulder completely heal. That left shoulder was Rogers's most precious commodity, yet he was willing to risk it because, in Cone's words, "I think Kenny wanted to prove to people that he wasn't some redneck who couldn't handle it in New York."

Many months later Rogers would admit, "I should've just shut myself down until my shoulder felt better. But I didn't. I was stupid." He proceeded to have an awful spring, sometimes throwing no better than eighty-one miles per hour. Every pitcher goes through what is called the "dead-arm period," when, in the first weeks following a winter of inactivity, the muscles surrounding the rotator cuff go into shock. Indeed, it's one of the passages of spring for a pitcher to lose his fastball and then, mysteriously, have it return.

Maybe in any other camp Rogers's rapidly inflating ERA could have been glossed over. But these were the Yankees, and he was learning fast that anxiety and tension were the organization's primary fuel. Torre had decisions, decisions: there were seven starters for five spots, and Rogers—regardless of the massive financial commitment Steinbrenner had made to him—wasn't helping himself with an ERA that, by the last week of camp, had risen to 8.48.

Somehow, Torre had to choose a starting five from a pool of Cone, Gooden, Pettitte, Key, Rogers, Melido Perez, and Scott Kamieniecki. There were two factors complicating Torre's thought process. First, Key was healing faster than anyone expected, and, second, Gooden, whose ERA was even higher than that of Rogers, was clearly Steinbrenner's personal reclamation project and therefore untouchable.

As for Kamieniecki . . . well, he was coming off elbow surgery from the previous winter and seemed like a long shot. And Perez had undergone surgery too but was pitching so well in camp that he was forcing himself into Torre's consciousness. Poor Rogers. He looked lost, sometimes even helpless, going into the final weekend of camp, when Torre faced his first crisis.

Rogers must have sensed something was wrong when he was intercepted by Reggie Jackson on his way to the clubhouse. Reggie, a middle-level adviser to Steinbrenner in the Showalter years, was now higher in the chain of command, having forged a personal relationship with Torre for so many years as one of his broadcasting partners in California.

Reggie now sat in on meetings, offered advice, and was allowed to walk about the clubhouse, "to be my liaison with the players," according to Torre—which was fine with Reggie, who missed the Yankee spotlight and was still looking for Steinbrenner to recognize him as a front-office force to be reckoned with.

"What I really want," Jackson said in a private moment one day, "is to be one of the vice presidents of this team. But George doesn't want it. Don't ask me why. He just doesn't respect me."

For now Reggie was dispatched by Torre to get Rogers and bring him into the manager's office, where Torre and Stottlemyre were waiting. And that is where Rogers heard the bad news: he was being sent to the bull pen. Kenny Rogers, the American League's second-winningest pitcher behind Randy Johnson between 1993 and 1995, a $20 million free agent, a seventeen-game winner, was suddenly a reliever. "This is not a punishment," Torre said, although you couldn't blame Rogers for believing otherwise. He stared straight ahead as he heard the pronouncement, answered a few questions from the press in what was barely more than a whisper, and decided it was better to keep his mouth shut altogether.

But it was clear Rogers's feelings were hurt. Two days later he told the *New York Post* that he felt like giving the $20 million back if that's how little Torre and the rest of the front office thought of him. That was just Rogers's temper boiling over, and his agent, Scott Boras, later said, "Kenny isn't really serious about giving back the contract. But he is wondering why he was suddenly being forced to audition for the starting rotation out of spring training."

It was an excellent point. But what else was Torre going to do? Key had pitched so well he was already part of the starting rotation, and Cone, Pettitte, and Gooden were safe. What Torre finally decided to do was to buy time. First, he placed Kamieniecki on the disabled list, then followed up by deciding to keep Perez in Florida when the Yankees went north.

In his last two starts, Perez had shown signs of a deteriorating elbow, reaching only the mid-eighties against the Cardinals and then still failing to break ninety mph during an intrasquad game on the last day of camp. One more time, Torre held an office summit. Perez, who was in the final year of his contract and on the doorstep of free agency, emerged from Torre's office with anger written all over his face.

He went to his locker, picked up his duffel bag, and sent it hurtling across the room. The bag nearly struck a Yankee intern in the head, then crashed into the side of a locker. "Yikes," Cone said quietly, as everyone turned his head away in embarrassment for Perez.

Incredibly, Rogers was back in the rotation, but he would make a few tune-up starts in Florida until the Yankees needed him in late April. The question was: What would the Yankees look like by that time? The eleventh hour at Legends Field was pure insanity, as Tony Fernandez broke his elbow diving for a pop fly, Pat Kelly reinjured his throwing shoulder, and Mariano Duncan became the only available second baseman.

For days, the Yankees tried to pry Chuck Knoblauch away from the Twins, failing outright. Then Tim Raines fractured his left thumb. It wasn't hard to see that the Yankees were missing right-handed power—Mike Stanley's home runs, to be exact—but over and over Torre kept saying, "It's going to be our pitching that'll carry us." It was a good Yankee team that left Tampa in April. Good, but not great, and certainly not anything near the star quotient of the Orioles. In fact, with the Red Sox loaded up with Mo Vaughn, Jose Canseco, and Kevin Mitchell, the Yankees were probably only the third-best on-paper team in the East. And why not?

There was a new manager in place, a complete stranger to the American League—just like the new general manager. Four fifths of the starting rotation consisted of a wobbly Kenny Rogers, a still recovering Key, a twice-suspended Doc Gooden, and second-year Andy Pettitte. All the Yankees could really count on was Cone

Was he ready? Were the Yankees?

"For better or worse," Cone said, "we're about to find out, aren't we?"

Mariano Rivera

3

Orioles-Yankees, Act I

O riole Park at Camden Yards is an exquisite ballpark, so perfect in every way that it makes George Steinbrenner crazy. He'd sooner give guided tours of the Bronx than be caught sitting in the company of his own hated rival, Peter Angelos, looking out across the gleaming ball field toward the city skyline that sits beyond the centerfield fence.

The place has everything George craves for his very own: the cash-cow luxury boxes, the downtown ambience, the luxury boxes, the fan-friendly concession areas, the luxury boxes, the traffic-friendly access to mass transit and major highways, and, oh yes, the luxury boxes.

To say nothing of the more than three million paying customers per season.

Of course, Yankee Stadium has unmatched ambience, not to mention a sacred tradition all its own. But in terms of the convenience and social atmosphere needed to attract the family entertainment dollar in the nineties, it is Coney Island while Camden Yards is Disney World.

And did we mention George's ballpark is short on luxury boxes?

Steinbrenner was angling for a new stadium before Camden Yards ever opened for business in 1992, but he became more obsessed with building a comparable palace after he got a look at Baltimore's new digs. The debate about traffic and parking and the neighborhood element around Yankee Stadium has fueled many an explosive hour on talk radio, and it's still anybody's guess where the Yankees will be playing when their lease in the Bronx runs out in six years.

Nothing short of a postseason matchup could get Steinbrenner to set foot on Angelos's turf until he has a Camden Yards he can call his very own. During the season he shows up from time to time in places like Chicago, Detroit, Toronto, Arlington, Minneapolis, Milwaukee, and Cleveland to watch his Yankees. He has even been to Boston now and then over the years. But he never goes to Baltimore.

He didn't get along with former Orioles owner Edward Bennett Williams, and he despises Angelos. The O's owner alienated his wealthy brethren by refusing to go along with the replacement-player scam during the players' strike in '94–'95, but Steinbrenner takes special exception, perhaps because Angelos is cut from the same mold in many ways and unquestionably because the new kid on the block has been outspoken about trying to overtake the Yankees as the premier franchise in baseball.

It was all part of the intrigue that had been building since the two owners began comparing the size of their wallets back in December. Steinbrenner's personal feelings aside, the Yankees-Orioles rivalry had gone flat over the last couple of decades because neither franchise had won a division title since 1983, the year the O's won it all.

But with stars on both sides now and the personal war being waged by the owners, an instant rivalry was created. And a month into the season, both sides were looking to draw first blood.

At the time neither side knew what to make of their ball clubs. The Orioles had slumped after a fast 11-2 start, and already there were signs of the internal turbulence that would trouble them all season.

The Yankees, meanwhile, were playing decent baseball but nothing that suggested grand possibilities. April had little of the poignancy that Dwight Gooden and David Cone would provide in May. Gooden's struggle as a starter in his first three would create talk of a return to the minor leagues and set the stage for his remarkable night of redemption in May, but the early weeks of the season would be remembered most for a couple of freaks of nature: first was the April snow that fell during the home opener; second was the emergence of Mariano Rivera.

By the time Joe DiMaggio launched the home opener with a ceremonial first pitch, the euphoria of a two-game sweep in Cleveland had been tempered by the three-game spanking the Yankees received in Texas.

Now, as snow fell throughout the day, the Yankees eased their way to a 7–3 victory over the Royals behind the pitching of Andy Pettitte. The snow made for good video, if not good baseball. No doubt the fans who filled the stadium will remember it as a howling blizzard as the years pass and the stories told to friends and family get slightly embellished.

Likewise, media members will be recounting the tale of the pregame fireworks they witnessed in the press dining room.

To the astonishment of one and all, Yankee PR adviser Arthur Richman unleashed six months of stored fury on Mike Lupica in a vulgar diatribe that included a threat to take Lupica out in the hallway and "wipe the concrete" with him.

Now, it's one thing for Bobby Bonilla to threaten to show a sportswriter the Bronx. Unpleasant as it may be, you figure it comes with the territory. A veteran sportswriter who has never had a serious run-in with a player is probably either working in San Diego or covering indoor soccer.

But it's quite something else to be taken to task in front of your peers by a seventy-year-old man. That Lupica, the most powerful columnist in the city, was on the receiving end only heightened the improbability, not to mention the spectacle. Indeed, no one could remember a scene quite like this.

It turned out that Richman had been waiting for this opportunity since Lupica labeled him a "bootlicker" in the *Daily News* back in November.

The source of conflict had been the change of managers. Lupica was passionate in his support of Buck Showalter, while it was Richman, a longtime friend of Joe Torre's, who recommended the hiring of Torre to George Steinbrenner.

It was also Richman who answered publicly for Steinbrenner when the Showalter dismissal erupted into a huge media firestorm. Did Buck walk away, as Steinbrenner insisted at the time, or was he effectively fired for refusing to sacrifice hitting coach Rick Down? The issue was debated hotly on WFAN for days in November. Richman defended Steinbrenner in an interview with Russ Salzberg and Steve Somers, the FAN morning team, saying that he had heard the final phone conversation between George and Buck while sitting in Steinbrenner's office. Richman, like Steinbrenner, insisted that Showalter had made it clear on the phone that he didn't want to return.

The interview with Salzberg and Somers was amicable, but Mike Francesa and Chris Russo proceeded to ridicule Richman that day on their afternoon show. How was it, they asked, that Richman could hear what Showalter was saying when the conversation wasn't on a speaker phone and Richman admitted he wasn't on another extension? Was he Superman? Did he have super hearing powers? During the interview Richman had also testified that Showalter wasn't nearly as squeaky-clean as his public image would indicate and brought Lupica's name into it by declaring that Lupica himself would be shocked to find out what the manager really thought of him.

Lupica, who has made villifying Steinbrenner a career, responded in his Sunday "Shooting from the Lip" column by discrediting Richman as nothing more than a Steinbrenner bootlicker. Richman, who has worked various baseball jobs for some fifty years and claims to have more friends in the game than any man alive, was irate. He planned to confront Lupica during spring training, but the columnist, in what amounted to a protest of Showalter's firing, refused to set foot in Tampa.

Finally, at the home opener, Richman had his chance. Lupica was having lunch, an hour or so before the ball game, when Richman marched over to his table and shattered the quiet hum of dining conversation with an explosion of profanity.

"You motherfucker, Lupica," Richman said, raising his voice. "Call me a bootlicker now, you motherfucker, and I'll take you outside and wipe the fuckin' concrete with you."

Forks came to a dead stop throughout the room. Heads turned, mouths agape. Computer keyboards went still in the adjoining pressroom, as writers composing pregame note packages heard the commotion and came scrambling to the door to bear witness.

Richman cared not at all that he was creating such an astonishing scene. Here was this grandfatherly little man railing at a columnist so influential that most people involved in New York sports avoided crossing him at all costs. Lupica, meanwhile, seemed stunned. He barely reacted, instead staring in disbelief from across the table.

Finally, after a solid couple of minutes of expletives, old Artie's face was flushed and everyone in the room was thinking his heart was going to give out on him any minute. But just then a couple of the Yankees' security people came scurrying to intervene and gently persuaded Richman to leave the room.

Lupica was both mortified and incensed. He didn't stay for the game, choosing instead to go outside and interview fans arriving at the stadium by subway. He wrote a column praising the fans for their loyalty to this franchise while taking Steinbrenner to task for playing the game in such miserable weather as well as for his very public desire for a new stadium.

The next day Lupica called interim commissioner Bud Selig, demanding an apology from Richman. American League spokeswoman Phyllis Merhige relayed the request, but it wasn't received terribly well.

Or as Richman proudly told acquaintances: "I told them they could go fuck themselves."

Finally, he was coerced into sending a written apology, though Lupica said it read more like a clarification of Richman's remarks than an apology. In any case, the incident only hardened the long-strained relationship between Lupica and Steinbrenner.

In years past The Boss was ever willing to make peace with his tormentor in the interest of more back-page attention. And likewise, if there was a good column in it for Lupica. But the Showalter firing and the Richman tirade, played against Lupica's stinging commentaries, embittered both sides to the point of no return.

The loathing came to a boil late in the season. On the day David Cone returned from his aneurysm surgery to pitch seven no-hit innings against the A's in Oakland, Lupica wanted to write a column chronicling the reaction of Cone's surgeon, Dr. George Todd. He called Todd's office and was told the Yankees had ordered Cone's doctors not to talk to the press.

Lupica then called the Yankees and told them to rescind the gag order or, rather than write a feel-good column about Cone's comeback, he'd blast them for their paranoid policies.

Steinbrenner's response was to organize a conference call with Todd for all interested media outlets—with one exception: no Lupica. In addition, Steinbrenner sent word to Lupica via a Yankee spokesman: "Don't threaten me."

Lupica sent word back telling Steinbrenner not to worry: "He'll know when I'm threatening him. And tell him if he doesn't knock it off, I'll start calling him a felon again in print."

Steinbrenner, you may recall, was convicted of a felony in 1972 for making illegal contributions to Richard Nixon's presidential campaign. Lupica for years wouldn't miss a chance to remind his readers of Steinbrenner's conviction, but a few years back he'd decided to invoke his own statute of limitations.

Now the gloves were off again, and, insults aside, the bottom line was that Lupica was slow to embrace this Yankee team as he had during the Showalter years. Maybe the public noticed, maybe it didn't. But the little war made for great intrigue in the press box. Would the Yankees win a championship? Would they win Lupica over? In New York both questions matter.

Three weeks after that memorable opening day, a championship seed was planted. A fireballing middle reliever came out of the bull pen to throw three hitless innings in a 6–2 win in Kansas City, and almost instantly the Super Mariano phenomenon was born.

Over the course of seven days, Mariano Rivera had striking impact on three different victories. On each occasion he pitched three hitless innings, once against the Royals and twice against the Twins. Two walks were all that separated Rivera from the equivalent of a perfect game.

Juiced-ball madness made it all the more remarkable. While scores all around the majors looked as if they belonged to a slow-pitch softball league, Rivera gave the Yankees the rarest of weapons—a middle-inning assassin.

"He should be in a higher league," Twins manager Tom Kelly said after watching Rivera blow his team away for the second time in three days. "Ban him from baseball. He should be illegal."

The Yankees had envisioned something like this the day they signed him as a nineteen-year-old free agent out of Panama. He threw ninety to ninety-one mph at the time, and his smooth, easy delivery made his lively fastball especially difficult for hitters to measure. During his first year in the minors, he gave up exactly one earned run in fifty-two innings of work.

His climb through the organization was delayed by elbow surgery in 1992, but he remained a prospect throughout. When the Yankees brought him up to make four starts in May of '95, however, they weren't terribly impressed. In need of pitching after Jimmy Key and Scott Kamieniecki were lost to injuries, the Yankees put Rivera into the rotation. He lost 10–3 to the A's in his major-league debut and went 1-2 with a 10.20 ERA in four starts, throwing mostly fastballs that were clocked on the Yankees' radar gun from eighty-nine to ninety-one mph. He looked as if he wasn't ready for the big leagues, and the Yankees sent him back to Columbus in early June.

It wasn't until then that Rivera told club officials his shoulder had been bothering him. After resting it for two weeks, he threw a five-inning, rain-shortened no-hitter for Columbus, during which he was clocked on the gun at ninety-five to ninety-six mph. When Gene Michael got the gun readings the next day, he was flabbergasted because Rivera had never thrown as hard as ninety-two mph on more than a couple of occasions.

Michael figured the readings had to be a mistake and called people in Columbus to double-check. When he was told they were right and assured the gun was working properly, Michael was still skeptical. He called a scout from a rival team who he knew had been in Columbus for the game and asked him what his readings were on Rivera. Again Michael was told they were ninety-five to ninety-six mph.

The general manager relayed the information to Buck Showalter that day, and they made plans to call up Rivera again. A week later he started against the White Sox and threw eight shutout innings, racking up eleven strikeouts. The numbers were for real, all right. Michael was not just delighted, he was relieved the Tigers hadn't stolen him.

For weeks Michael had been talking to Tigers general manager Joe Klein about a possible trade for David Wells. The Tigers, looking to dump Wells's $3 million salary, were looking for a top prospect or two from a contender. Michael offered Brian Boehringer, but the Tigers weren't interested. Klein asked about Rivera, and Michael said he was willing to discuss the possibility.

"I never said yes, and I never said no," Michael recalled a year later, smiling sheepishly. "I'm glad I never had to. They thought they could get more than that for Wells. Then when Rivera started throwing ninety-five, it was too late. Nobody was going to get him."

The Tigers wound up dealing Wells to the Cincinnati Reds for C. J. Nitkowski, a left-hander who had been a first-round draft pick out of St. John's in 1994. The Yanks wound up counting their blessings.

"I still don't know why it happened," Michael said of Rivera's increased velocity. "Maybe it took him that long for his arm to feel strong after he had the elbow problem. Maybe it was his shoulder. He was always very thin—maybe he just got a little bigger and stronger. Whatever it was, it made him a different pitcher."

Rivera couldn't quite harness his newfound velocity, however, and soon after his eleven-strikeout performance, he was moved to the bull pen, where he spent the rest of the season. But he continued to offer glimpses of his brilliance, particularly in the play-offs, when he relieved David Cone with the score tied in game five against the Mariners and struck out Mike Blowers to escape a bases-loaded jam and allow the Yankees to take their season into extra innings.

Besides temporarily rescuing the Yankees' season, that strikeout hit onlooking baseball executives like a lightning bolt. General managers everywhere reached for their voice recorders and dictated an urgent mental note: Find a way to get this kid.

Other general managers knew Michael to be a shrewd talent evaluator and careful deal maker who wasn't going to be suckered by the kind of marquee names that might tempt George Steinbrenner. But when Stick stepped down as general manager rather than take a pay cut, the vultures circled, preparing to swoop down on the Yankee front-office chaos. Some figured they could take advantage of Bob Watson's lack of familiarity with Rivera, but he read the reports and quickly decided Rivera was untouchable. He would say that between the winter and spring training he turned away as many as twenty offers from teams interested in Rivera.

"It would have had to be a great, great deal to even consider it," Watson would say.

And yet as the '96 season began there was no hint of the impact Rivera would have. He hadn't thrown the ball exceptionally well in spring training and didn't even figure into the late-inning bull-pen plans. Torre went in counting on Jeff Nelson, Steve Howe, and John Wetteland as his finishers and regarded Rivera as something of a spare tire, to be used in long relief or, if necessary, as a spot starter.

Two weeks into the season, in fact, Torre used Rivera to relieve Dwight Gooden in the fourth inning of an April 19 7–1 loss to the Twins. But after the three spectacular outings in late April, it was clear the Yankees had something special. The question was how to best utilize him.

There was some sentiment within the organization to make him a starter since Gooden was looking like a bust and Scott Kamieniecki was again having elbow problems. Torre took one look around his new league, however, and saw a better option. With the explosion of offense that was making quality starts a rarity, more and more games were being decided in the sixth and seventh innings at the expense of mediocre middle relief.

Rivera could be the kind of bridge from starter to closer that virtually no one else had. And since hitters rarely would get more than one look at that sneaky fastball if Rivera was limited to short bursts of pitching, the role suited him perfectly.

"I saw him as my wild card," Torre would say late in the season. "But even after those first early outings, I never could have predicted how much he would mean to us."

It wasn't until May 5 that Rivera so much as gave up another hit. A single by Chicago White Sox outfielder Tony

Phillips ended Rivera's hitless streak at fifteen innings, but his scoreless streak continued for another two weeks before ending at twenty-six innings.

Rivera's streak was still intact when the Yankees reached Baltimore for their first meeting with the Orioles, on April 30 and May 1. Already his emergence as a complement to John Wetteland was giving the Yankees a certain aura, providing the kind of late-inning bull-pen firepower that has often proved crucial to building a championship team.

It would turn out to be especially vital in the season-long domination by the Orioles. But it didn't begin to explain the first go-round between the teams. Going in, the Yankees regarded the two games as something of a measuring stick. They were a half game behind the first-place O's, but with a record of 12-10 the Yanks had yet to establish their own sense of where they were headed.

They were a high-priced collection of talent in search of an identity, but two seemingly endless nights later they felt like a unit. For grit, as much as anything, prevailed as the Yankees and Orioles played two games that totaled twenty-four innings and lasted nearly ten hours combined.

First, they set a record for the longest nine-inning game in major-league history, trading punches for four hours and twenty-one minutes as the Yankees came back from a 9–4 deficit to win, 13–10. Yet that turned out to be a mere warm-up for the second game, a fifteen-inning affair on a chilly, rainy night the Yankees finally won, 11–6.

"These were two games I'll never forget," Joe Torre said after the second night. "People asked about our leadership and what kind of ball club we were going to be. But after these two games I don't think anybody can question the chemistry, class, and ruggedness of this team. These games were special."

The wins, by the same token, were improbable. Consider that Andy Pettitte was knocked out in the second inning the first night and wound up coming back to pitch three shutout innings to earn the win the second night.

Or that Gerald Williams, of all people, became only the second Yankee ever to collect six hits in a game—the immortal Myril Hoag did it first, in 1934—as he fueled the offense in the second game. But if anyone personified the spirit of the two wins, it was a twenty-five-year-old pitcher named Jim Mecir, who had all of four innings of experience in the majors. Recalled from Triple A Columbus that very day to give the Yankees an extra arm in the bull pen after the first marathon, Mecir pitched three scoreless innings, escaping trouble in each, including one seemingly deadly jam.

With the bases loaded and two outs, Mecir fell behind 3-and-0 on Brady Anderson, who was off to a scorching start at the plate, tied for the league lead with twelve home runs. Yet Mecir came back to strike him out, finishing him off by getting Anderson to chase his off-speed fork ball, which tumbled from the thighs to the ankles as it crossed the plate.

"Mecir was the star," Torre said.

It wouldn't be enough to keep the kid in the big leagues for long, but it was enough to help launch a championship run.

Finally, there was Tino Martinez, who won his pinstripes as Mattingly's successor in this series, hitting game-winning home runs each night. He broke a 9–9 tie the first night with a three-run blast to right-center off Keith Shepherd in the seventh inning, then broke an 11–11 tie the second night with an opposite-field grand slam off Jimmy Myers.

That second night Martinez seemed to sense the significance of the moment, both for him as a player trying to turn the boos of Mattingly fans to cheers and for a team just beginning to mesh as a contender. In a giddy clubhouse it was Martinez who offered the most relevant perspective.

"It takes time to come together and find an identity, and I think we did that," he said. "Once you establish yourself as a team that never gives up, that's what wins championships."

On the other hand, all the Orioles were establishing was something of a Bronx Zoo South. In Davey Johnson's first year as manager, the O's were fast building an identity reminiscent of the last Yankee championship ball club, the turbulent mix of Reggie and Billy and Thurman and George that produced back-to-back World Series winners in 1977 and '78.

Bobby Bonilla already had been complaining for weeks about being used as a designated hitter, and he was up to his old Met tricks with the media. When Baltimore *Sun* columnist Ken Rosenthal suggested in print that Bonilla keep an open mind about designated hitting since it would best serve the team, Bobby Bo confronted Rosenthal and warned him:

"Don't come by my locker or I'll shove my foot up your ass."

But Bonilla carried little weight in the Orioles' clubhouse. The influence belonged to Cal Ripken, Jr., the man given credit for saving baseball in the poststrike season of '95. His breaking of Lou Gehrig's Iron Man record for consecutive games played was a celebration of the work ethic, the very antithesis of baseball's image in the wake of its labor war between millionaires.

Oriole managers had been careful not to tamper with history during Ripken's chase. But the streak was in the books now, and Davey Johnson was more interested in taking the O's back to the postseason for the first time since 1983.

And it was Ripken, after all, who insisted the streak was nothing more than a sincere effort to give his team its best chance to win every night. So Johnson gave it little thought when he pulled Ripken for a pinch runner in the eighth inning of the second game with the Yankees in this series.

The O's were down a run at the time and Manny Alexander had a much better chance of scoring from first on a double than Ripken did. Never mind that Alexander got picked off and the game wound up going another seven innings; from a win-the-game perspective it was a no-brainer. It wasn't as if he was messing with the streak anyway.

But since the streak had begun thirteen years ago, Ripken had never been replaced at such a meaningful moment of a ball game. He looked startled when he saw Alexander heading his way, as though he didn't understand what was happening. Then, as he jogged to the dugout, a hush seemed to come over the crowd. This wasn't going unnoticed in the stands, to say nothing of the press box. Ripken hadn't even reached the dugout yet and Baltimore reporters were on the phone, calling their editors with news that would shake the city.

The move created such a media frenzy that Johnson would say, "It was like I was impeaching the president."

Ripken, of course, could have made it a nonissue by acknowledging the manager's right to try to win the game. Instead, after sitting solemnly in the dugout through the final innings, his postgame reaction forecast trouble in Birdland.

"I don't wish to make a comment one way or the other," Ripken told the salivating reporters at his locker. "I'll just let that stand as my response."

Loose translation: Davey Johnson is a peabrain.

His response was transparent enough. Judging by talk radio, reaction in Baltimore was split. Some fans were shocked that Saint Cal had such a selfish side. Others defended his reaction as part of the competitive drive that allowed him to break the unbreakable record.

One thing for sure: Davey would not be welcome in the back of the plane, having a beer and playing a hand of cards with this team as he once had with the Mets in the eighties. Ripken set the tone in the O's clubhouse, and his resentment toward Johnson became contagious.

It would grow closer to mutiny in the coming weeks when Johnson announced his intention to move Ripken to third base in the absence of injured B. J. Surhoff.

Ripken again took subtle jabs at Johnson rather than openly express his anger. But he stopped talking to Manny Alexander, the kid who would play short during the move.

Meanwhile, Cal confidants Brady Anderson, Mike Mussina, and Scott Erickson were quietly outraged. Bonilla, as usual, wasn't quiet at all, telling Baltimore reporters that Johnson "has a lot to answer for around here."

It wasn't helping Johnson that he was keeping short hours. Managers make a habit of being in their office at least five hours before game time, at least for night games, but some days Johnson was rolling in right off the golf course just as batting practice was starting about 5 P.M. In a sport where the work ethic is considered essential to succeeding across a 162-game season, Davey was sending a dangerous message.

But Johnson seemed unfazed by the winds of controversy he was stirring. By winning a division title with the Reds in 1995, he'd regained the status he'd lost when he couldn't get a job for three years after being fired by the Mets. No longer was he haunted by whispers that he was drinking too much or running wild at night.

Remarried after a divorce, he was not quite the brash Davey who once cast the Mets as villains by saying he expected them to dominate the National League in 1986, which they did. But he was as cocksure of his ability to evaluate talent and make decisions as he'd ever been. Mets fans may well have roared with laughter listening to Davey insist one day in the spring that Gregg Jefferies would have made a helluva second baseman if only the Mets had left him there like he told them.

As for the turmoil, Johnson seemed to relish a little give-and-take with his players.

Perhaps the Ripken fallout reminded him of those rollicking days with the Mets when he was challenging Darryl Strawberry to a fistfight or trading barbs through the newspapers with Ron Darling.

"Some of the best teams I ever had," Johnson defiantly told reporters, "you'd have thought were time bombs ready to go off. Sometimes it's good for a team to be on edge."

It remained to be seen, but a month into the season the identities were taking shape in remarkably contrasting forms. The Yankees were the definition of calm, thriving under the relaxed rein of their manager. And the Orioles were a mess.

David Cone

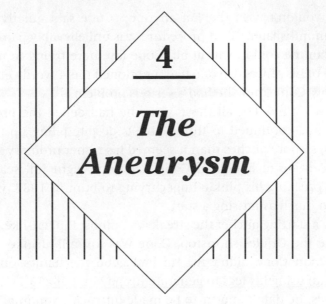

4

The Aneurysm

T he minutes lasted hours, the hours lasted days. David Cone had long since lost all sense of time as he lay in the hospital bed, drifting in and out of consciousness as he underwent an angiogram for the second time in ten days. The pain was torturous, coming in waves as doctors repeatedly injected dye into a catheter that snaked from Cone's groin up to and around his heart valves and back down to his right hand.

The injection of the dye—as well as an enzyme, urokinase, that is used to dissolve blood clots—caused a burning sensation that all but lifted Cone off the bed in pain.

How long could it go on? Cone wouldn't know until days later that the catheter had remained inside him for forty hours straight as doctors examined every inch of his body. He was groggy and exhausted. The pain made it impossible to sleep, but the combination of painkillers and a local anesthetic made it just as hard to stay coherent.

"I wouldn't wish that on anyone," Cone said quietly one day, months later. "That procedure was unbelievably painful."

When he could focus at all, Cone lay there trying to make sense of his ordeal. No one had mentioned the *A* word yet, but by now Cone knew he had a serious problem.

How? Why? For all those years he had defied the predictions and continued to throw bullets despite piling up more innings, more pitches than it seemed his rather ordinary body was capable of handling. Cone had gone eight full seasons since breaking his pinkie finger trying to bunt in 1987, without so much as missing a start.

For a starting pitcher the streak was almost Ripken-like, but, unlike the Orioles shortstop, Cone was no milk drinker. No, Iron Man Cone didn't fit. He had good mechanics on the mound, using his legs to generate his power, but at 5'11", 180 pounds, he didn't appear to be made for such pounding. And Mr. Fitness he was not. He'd thrown down his share of beers over the years, and for too long he'd been smoking more cigarettes than he cared to admit.

Yet his arm never failed him. It reached a point where Cone joked about his remarkable endurance. He didn't even bother to ice his arm after starts—near heresy these days.

"I believe in internal icing," Cone said one day in September of '95 after a big win, taking a swig of beer to illustrate his point. "It works for me."

But now the laughter had given way to agony. Was this the price he finally had to pay for those high pitch counts? Was it all over? So many thoughts flashed in and out of Cone's mind as he rode the pain roller-coaster, trying to think straight between the ups and downs of the medication.

Had one pitch done it? Had those 147 pitches in game five against the Mariners last October triggered the problem? Cone didn't know. The doctors would tell him that they'd never know for sure.

Cone couldn't help recalling that he'd never felt quite right throughout spring training. It took him more time than usual to get loose—first just to throw in camp and then to pitch in exhibition games.

At the time he tried not to dwell on it. At age thirty-four he wasn't a kid any longer. It wasn't supposed to be easy after ten years in the big leagues, was it? He'd take it slow, no sense overdoing it in the spring. He'd build toward April, wait for adrenaline to take over. And, he reminded himself more than once as he tried to shake the cobwebs from his shoulder during those six weeks in Tampa, he had to try to quit the damn cigarettes.

It wasn't only that his arm hurt. Something just wasn't quite the same. So while reporters peppered him with questions all spring about a fastball that landed in the catcher's glove with a pfft instead of a pop, Cone kept them at arm's length with the usual veteran jibberjab about the meaninglessness of spring-training results.

He didn't necessarily believe the words coming out of his mouth, but, sure enough, Cone went out in the season opener and made it all look easy again. He dominated the American League champion Indians in their ballpark to kick off the Yankees' season with an emotional win and reassure New Yorkers that all was well.

Yet it was after that game that Cone first noticed the numbness in his pitching hand. Initially, he thought little of it. The frosty thirty-eight-degree temperature in Cleveland made numbness seem perfectly normal. But as he sat in the trainer's room the numbness lingered, specifically in his right ring finger. From the knuckle to the fingertip "it was completely cold and lifeless," Cone would recall. He looked down to see that the nail on that finger was a frightening shade of blue.

When it persisted over his next couple of starts, he entered Columbia Presbyterian Medical Center in upper Manhattan for a first angiogram.

Afterward there was no mention of an aneurysm. Doctors hadn't detected it because, they later told Cone, the aneurysm's location made it difficult to see on the angiogram. Instead, they thought he had a circulation problem that was limited to his hand area. They couldn't identify the exact cause but told him it was good news—no blood clots, no problem with his arm. They put him on blood thinners and told him to limit his caffeine and stop drinking and smoking.

"I'm going to have to change my whole lifestyle," Cone joked at the time.

Five days later, on May 2, he went out and blew away the White Sox, pitching a complete-game five-hitter in a 5–1 win. Yet the numbness persisted.

Doctors ordered him to return to the hospital for a more extensive angiogram. He was admitted on Monday, May 6. A day later the mood was dark in the clubhouse as the Yankees prepared for a night game against the Detroit Tigers and awaited word on their ace. Amid speculation among the players that Cone had a blood clot, they seemed to be bracing for the worst.

"This isn't a sore shoulder," Wade Boggs said. "This is deadly serious."

Less than an hour before the game, Yankee team physician Stuart Hershon arrived at the stadium to tell the Yankees that doctors had found an aneurysm in the pitcher's arm. Cone would need surgery and probably would be out for the season.

Hershon huddled with Joe Torre and Bob Watson in the manager's office some forty-five minutes before game time.

Torre and Watson decided it would be best to wait until after the game for Hershon to tell the team. After the Yankees defeated the Tigers, 5–1, the players gathered around the doctor. Cone was immensely popular in all corners of the clubhouse, and more than a few teammates choked up as Hershon explained the situation.

"There were a lot of glassy eyes," Torre recalled later in the season. "It was very emotional."

It was devastating as well. The news paralyzed the organization. No one believed for a second that the Yankees could survive an extended loss of Cone, and now it seemed unlikely he would be back at all in '96. The strain was such that the normally unshakable Torre lost his cool with the media after the game.

During the game word of the aneurysm had filtered through the press box, sending everyone scrambling for medical dictionaries for a definition of the term. No one was bothering to watch the game—it would be little more than a footnote compared to the Cone story.

Finally it ended and reporters hustled into Torre's office. You never expect detailed explanations of anything at Yankee Stadium, but reporters figured at least to get a clear understanding of what an aneurysm was and what it meant to Cone. It turned out that was expecting far too much.

In Torre's office PR director Rick Cerrone introduced Hershon, who stood near the manager's desk next to Bob Watson. Hershon cleared his throat uncomfortably and announced that Cone had an aneurysm in his arm.

"We picked this up early," said Hershon. "That's the good news. We feel this is correctable and not career-threatening."

With that, Hershon said he would neither answer questions nor offer any further details at this time.

"Can you at least tell us what an aneurysm is?" someone shouted at Hershon.

"I'm not going to answer questions at this time," Hershon said nervously, looking as if he feared Steinbrenner was listening in on an intercom somewhere.

"Will he be able to pitch again this season?" someone else asked.

"I'm not going to get into that at this time," Hershon said.

The grumbling was beginning to build. This was no time to be humping the press corps, at eleven o'clock at night with deadlines hovering and editors in the office demanding details on the biggest story of the season to date. Most reporters understood this wasn't Hershon's call so much as typical protocol in an organization whose employees live in fear of being fired for saying anything that might not meet the owner's approval.

But Joel Sherman of the *Post* wasn't in the mood for courtesies.

"Then why are you even here?" he blurted at Hershon, stinging the good doctor with a jab that silenced the room.

Torre, sitting at his desk at the time, was apart from the discussion. But now he quickly returned fire on Sherman.

"Because if he wasn't here you'd have something else to fucking bitch about."

The words were cold, the tone was harsh. Writers looked at one another in disbelief: What's up with Gentleman Joe?

By now the New York press regarded Torre as a godsend, the rare manager who answered tough questions without rancor, a man secure enough in his ability that he addressed delicate issues with remarkable frankness, seemingly without fear of Steinbrenner reprimands.

But Torre had a hard edge that showed now and then. A couple of weeks earlier he had stunned radio analyst Michael

Kay by challenging him in the middle of the clubhouse a couple of hours before a game.

"You and I have a problem," Torre said to Kay. "I don't need any Rona Barretts in my clubhouse."

Kay was startled. He knew this had to be about Paul O'Neill. The night before, Torre had replaced O'Neill with Gerald Williams in the ninth inning of a 10–8 victory over the Cleveland Indians. It was unusual, since O'Neill rarely comes out for defensive reasons. But a day earlier the manager had said he thought O'Neill should have caught a fly ball that fell in for a double in a 5–2 loss in Kansas City.

So Kay, who does postgame interviews with a camera crew for the MSG network, asked Torre on camera if he was sending a message to O'Neill. Torre said no, that wasn't the case, adding, "I'm a Paul O'Neill fan. He works as hard as anybody. I wish they were all like Paul."

But apparently he thought Kay was trying to create a rift between him and one of his players. Or maybe, with the O'Neill story all over the papers, Torre just wanted a way to show his players he was in their corner. It looked that way as he confronted Kay and put on a show in the middle of the clubhouse, yelling loudly enough for his players to hear.

The more Kay tried to reason with Torre, the louder the manager became. Finally Kay stopped debating the point and Torre walked away as players watched from their lockers.

A half-hour later, as the Yankees took batting practice, Kay confronted Torre on the field.

"There's gotta be something deeper here, Joe," Kay said. "I want to know what it is."

"I don't trust you," said Torre.

"Why, what have I done?" Kay asked.

"It's just a feeling I have," said Torre.

Kay didn't believe him. It was no secret that Kay had been tight with Buck Showalter, and he figured somebody in the organization must have been whispering such things to Torre. But when Kay tried to pursue the point, Torre just walked away.

The next day Torre was friendly toward Kay, with no hint anything had happened between them. Kay didn't back off, continuing to ask Torre pertinent questions after games about strategy and lineup decisions. And the manager answered with his typical candor. The two of them didn't have a problem the rest of the year.

But Torre had made his point and established the ground rules. As accommodating as he could be with the press, Torre could be fiercely protective of the people around him. In this case, with emotions running high in the wake of the Cone news, he didn't like the idea of a wise-guy reporter embarrassing the team doctor, and he let Sherman know about it.

"All I'm trying to do is get a definition of what an aneurysm is," Sherman protested.

"Go look it up in a medical dictionary," Torre snapped.

"I did. But I'd like to have a doctor explain it. Just like, when I watch a baseball game, I think I know what I'm seeing but I like to ask the manager to explain why certain things happened."

"Yeah," snarled Torre, "and then you go and write whatever the fuck you want to write anyway."

By now everyone in the room was squirming uncomfortably, wanting this to end. Torre's outburst barely registered on the Billy Martin scale of scathing media abuse, but no one had seen this side of him. Even Sherman, perhaps the most contentious reporter in the city, seemed stunned and diplomatically ended the exchange by saying it wasn't the time or the place, especially with deadlines approaching.

An awkward silence hung in the air for a moment as Torre continued to pierce Sherman with his stare, but other reporters jumped in quickly, peppering both Torre and Watson with questions about how they would handle life without their ace.

Cone himself needed a day to absorb the news, shake off the wooziness from the painkillers, and recover from the angiogram.

Aneurysm? The word sent chills through Cone and his wife, Lynn. Like most people, they associated it with death, or at least serious illness, because they'd heard it so rarely. In fact, an aneurysm is a ballooning of an artery that results when diseases or injury weaken the inner lining of a blood vessel. They can occur anywhere in the body but most commonly involve the heart or the brain, which is why it's rare the word is used outside the medical community unless describing a life-threatening or even fatal condition.

But wherever aneurysms occur, blood clots can form as a result, blocking blood flow and even causing the artery to burst.

In Cone's case, doctors felt the aneurysm resulted from the mechanical stress of his pitching motion, though they couldn't point to a specific cause. The force of his motion was squeezing the aneurysm, pushing out blood clots that lodged in smaller arteries in Cone's hand area, causing the circulation problems. Had the aneurysm not been treated, it may have burst at some point and Cone could have lost part of his arm.

So three days after the angiogram, he underwent three hours of surgery at Columbia Presbyterian. Surgeons cut two arteries, removed the aneurysm, and performed a graft using a piece of vein from Cone's left thigh to restore the connection and the blood flow.

Fortunately for Cone, doctors were able to cut through the armpit area to get to the aneurysm. The throwing muscles in his shoulder were undisturbed by the surgery; otherwise he would have been finished for the season. As it was, the Yankees didn't actually expect to see him pitch again in '96.

But Cone was determined. Five days after the surgery, he convinced doctors to allow him to stop by Yankee Stadium on his way home from the hospital so he could publicly thank fans for their support and let people know he was okay. It turned out to be an emotional press conference as the weeks of anxiety, even fear, coupled with a sense of thanks that his career hadn't been taken from him, spilled into tears.

"It was a little overwhelming," Cone would say later.

From the stadium Cone went home to his Manhattan apartment to recuperate. But at the same time, his father-in-law was dying of lung cancer, taking a turn for the worse the very week Cone was discharged from the hospital. So the day after the press conference Cone and Lynn drove to Branford, Connecticut, to be with her father.

"That was an incredibly difficult time emotionally," Cone said later in the season. "I was drained and very emotional. I had pitching taken away from me for the first time, and that was emotional in itself. I was so used to being in control of my life and my career. That was a huge letdown, and then to see my father-in-law on his deathbed, it was unbelievably difficult."

His father-in-law wound up dying of lung cancer in July, by which time Cone was working out, pushing himself for a comeback. He was under strict orders not to throw hard for three months, the time doctors declared necessary for the vein graft to heal fully. But as the weeks passed, Cone was surprised at how good and strong he felt physically.

And gradually the emotional terror of the nightmare was passing. He was jolted, however, three weeks after the surgery by a story in *The New York Times*. Written by Lawrence K. Altman, the *Times*'s medical reporter and a doctor himself, the story cited anonymous sources at Columbia Presbyterian as saying at least one doctor suspected an aneurysm after the first angiogram but didn't act to warn or even stop Cone from making that subsequent start against the White Sox.

Shaken initially, Cone eventually found it hard to believe the story was true. Still, he had trouble dismissing it.

"I don't know what to believe, I honestly don't," Cone said after he'd resumed pitching. "I never heard anything from that doctor, whoever he is. Several doctors saw the angiogram. But they all knew I was pitching that night. Why wouldn't he have come to me and said, 'Wait a minute, I think I saw something?' If it's true, I'll never understand that scenario."

As the weeks passed and Cone came back to take the mound again in late August, the aneurysm and all its fallout would haunt him less and less. He quickly focused on the comeback, grateful that his arm was feeling better than he could have imagined. Doctors assured him the vein graft made his arm stronger than ever, that the odds of a recurrence were very, very long. But in some ways he would be forever changed. How close had he come to tragedy? One more start? A couple? For Cone, even months after he first heard the word "aneurysm," it was hard not to wonder.

Dwight Gooden

5

The Doctor Is In

There they were, two cross-town ghosts from the eighties. The road from Yankee Stadium to Shea Stadium is just about a straight shot: only a few miles down the Major Deegan Expressway to the Triboro Bridge, pay the toll, onto the Grand Central Parkway, past LaGuardia, and right into Shea's waiting arms. Without traffic, an aggressive cabby can make it in less than fifteen minutes.

But the gulf between the Yankees and the Mets is far, far greater than any short car ride. For a Met to become a Yankee—to go from ultrahip to ultratradition—was almost unthinkable a decade ago, certainly for two of its biggest stars, David Cone and Dwight Gooden. Cone and Gooden, the two Cy Young Award winners who embodied all that the eighties Mets were about—and the Yankees were not. One threw the unhittable gas, the other had more pitches than he could count on one hand. For a time, it seemed as if Gooden and

Cone would rule Shea, if not the baseball world, well into the nineties.

Of course, it never happened that way. The Mets traded away Cone in 1992, convinced he was the anonymous source in so many newspaper stories—"One Met Said," the club execs called him—that were part of the franchise's downfall. And Doc had already lost his fastball by 1994, when he suffered a stunning series of setbacks in his struggle with cocaine addiction. Out of baseball for all of 1995, Gooden finally committed himself to a 12-Step Narcotics Anonymous program in St. Petersburg, spent the entire summer auditioning for major-league scouts, and landed with the Yankees in November 1995.

Gooden could still remember that final meeting with George Steinbrenner, sitting across from him at the Bay Harbor Inn in Tampa. Doc, his father, Dan, and his adviser, Ray Negron, were about to shake hands on a $1 million deal for 1996, with a $2 million option for 1997 and a $3 million option for 1998, before The Boss said, "You better not make me look bad, Dwight. You do, and I swear you'll regret you ever met me."

There was a silence in the room before Gooden finally extended his hand. There had been other interested teams: the Red Sox, the White Sox, and especially the Marlins, who, by offering $1.5 million for '95, had actually outbid the Yankees by $500,000. Gooden was tempted by the lure of playing on the same team as his nephew Gary Sheffield, not to mention the scores of relatives who would be able to watch him on a daily basis.

In fact, it was Doc's long-range plan to sign a two-year deal somewhere, then finish out his career with the expansion Tampa Bay Devil Rays, a mere eight miles from his home. But there was still something about pitching for the Yankees that seduced Gooden. Had it been watching the play-offs a month earlier? The possibility of being reunited with Cone and maybe even Darryl Strawberry? Or was it a chance to have a last laugh on Mets general manager Frank Cashen?

"All those things ran through my mind, but mostly it was about coming back to New York," Gooden said. "This is the place where I started my career and then got hurt. This is the place I wanted to finish it. I wanted to show people I wasn't a failure. I wanted to show my kids that I was a big enough man to come back."

Sheffield had made one last attempt to steer Gooden clear of the Bronx. In a telephone conversation, the Marlins slugger said, "How can you go back there, with all the problems you had in New York the first time? All those leeches are gonna be back, Doc."

At this Gooden just laughed. "Cuz, you know that if I'm gonna mess up, it doesn't matter where I am. Besides, every time I ever started using, it's been in Florida, not New York."

Gooden was right about that: both his lapses in 1987 and 1994 took place in Tampa, where he said the nightlife turned him into "some kind of vampire." So, Gooden asked himself, what did it matter if he signed with the Yankees or not? At least he'd have a chance to resurrect his career in the biggest market of all and prove to all those critics that even the most disgraced athlete deserves a second chance.

One of Gooden's enemies was Met manager Dallas Green, who had offered little sympathy when Doc went down in '94 to cocaine. In fact, Green went as far as to say that Gooden had not only sabotaged himself but the team as well and that drug use was a matter of choice, not addiction.

For three years, the fire of revenge smoldered within Gooden. Privately, he told a reporter, "Dallas will get his one of these days. I haven't forgotten what he said about me. The way he drinks . . . believe me, he's got his own problems. But I'll wait."

Gooden seemed to understand his own vulnerability, at least in the first few days of camp. Better to keep his mouth shut, pitch well, make the team, and repay old debts later. For now, it was enough just to get used to the look and feel of pin-stripes. Not just for Gooden but Cone, too, side by side on a Tampa pitching mound, reliving the old days.

Actually, there were quite a few differences from the golden era at Shea. For one, Cone was throwing barely eighty-two mph, this being his first attempt to reheat the right arm after that devastating game five loss to the Mariners. After 147 pitches on October 8, Cone was so exhausted his wife, Lynn, said, "David spent about a week on the living-room couch after that game. He looked so pale, I was starting to worry."

No question, Cone was paying the price for all the innings, all those splitters. And so was Gooden. No longer was the one-time strikeout deity a lean assembly of arms and legs. Doc had grown thicker and stronger over the years, and, walking to the mound, he had the rolling gait of a football running back. The metamorphosis showed in his delivery too. Back in the eight-ies, Gooden was so thin-limbed, his left leg would almost reach toward his chin before he let loose with another unhit-table fastball.

But now in 1996, Gooden barely brought his leg higher than belt level. "Just can't work it like I used to. My damned legs are too big now," Doc would say with a laugh. Still, it was obvious Gooden had trained hard in the off season and had come to camp well ahead of the other pitchers. Cone, in fact, watched in disbelief as Gooden threw one ninety-plus fastball after another, while he continued to struggle in the low eighties.

"Right there, I knew Doc was serious about his comeback," Cone said. "I saw him throwing hard—real gas, on the very first day. Hell, he made me feel pretty inadequate."

But as Gooden was to learn the hard way, there's more to a baseball life than velocity. While it was true that Doc could still reach into the nineties, no small feat for a pitcher in his thirties, it was also obvious that he didn't have much last-second explosion in his heater. It wasn't like the Shea Stadium fastball he used to throw, which would look so appetizing to hitters for the first fifty-five feet to the plate, then rise, almost to the eyes, at the last second.

Hitters would tell each other to stay away from Doc's high heat. But who could resist a fastball at belt level? That was his magic, which, somehow, had deserted him. Gooden might have looked and sounded impressive on the sidelines in Tampa, as pitch after pitch thundered into Joe Girardi's glove, but facing hitters was another matter.

In fact, the spring turned out to be one long disaster for Gooden. He finished with an 8.88 ERA, and opponents batted .314 against him. In his final start before the regular season, the Pirates pummeled him for eight runs and fourteen hits, including three home runs, in just five innings. And while Bucs manager Jim Leyland tried his best to be diplomatic about embarrassing Gooden—Leyland actually said, "The wind carried a couple of those balls out of here"—there was no denying how just badly the Yankees seemed to have miscalculated.

After all, it was George Steinbrenner who had predicted Gooden would be a fifteen-game winner and called on him to be a team leader. Now it would be a moral victory for Gooden just to be the number-five pitcher. It was a sad sight to see, Gooden standing in the middle of the tiny visitors' clubhouse in Bradenton, the sweat still dripping off him, an aging pitcher failing to see that he'd become so hittable.

"I'm not worried. I've just got to keep working on my mechanics, make sure I stay back, not rush" is how Gooden put it. Was this noble experiment over? Gooden had earned the respect of the Yankees for his commitment to sobriety, but, with the regular season only days away, Torre had to decide how much Gooden could actually help his team.

Ultimately, Torre decided to keep Gooden in the rotation long enough for Kenny Rogers to work himself into shape. That meant three more starts, all of which were colossal failures. The Rangers routed Gooden twice in less than a week, and, in his third start on April 19, the Twins scored six runs in just three innings. That swelled Gooden's ERA to 11.48 and forced Torre to state the obvious.

"I don't like what I'm seeing from Doc," the manager said. "He doesn't seem to have a lot of self-confidence right now." And with that, Torre suggested that Gooden restore his mechanics in the zero-pressure confines of long relief.

It was a bitter pill for Gooden to swallow—the youngest Cy Young Award winner in baseball history being put out to pasture. Publicly, Gooden made sure to say all the right things about helping the team any way he could, but his embarrassment was profound. In fact, Gooden implored his adviser, Negron, who had since become a Yankee consultant, to "get me out of here."

Indeed, there had been some talk of sending Gooden to Triple A. Gooden told Negron that not only would he refuse such a request if General Manager Bob Watson made it, but he would then ask for his outright release. Doc said, "No fucking way that I'm going to Columbus. You know how those things go: once you're down in the minors, you never come back. It's like the end of your career. If I can't pitch here, I'm sure there's someone out there who'd take a chance on me."

It wasn't hard to understand Gooden's frustration, but the Yankees weren't his problem. It was his delivery, which, in retrospect, was choking the life out of his fastball. In the following week, Gooden did little more than play catch with Mel

Stottlemyre, his old friend and pitching coach from the Mets. Stottlemyre was just as mystified as anyone else in the Yankee brain trust by Gooden's evaporation, but, in the back of his mind, he was wondering about an unconscious habit Gooden once had as a Met.

When warming up in the bull pen, Gooden would take his natural, massive windup, the arms and legs so masterfully hiding the ball from the hitter until the last second. But just as the national anthem was playing, when Gooden had less than thirty seconds to be on the field, he would hurry up and eliminate most of the leg kick and arm swing from the delivery, just so he could squeeze in a few more pitches. And that's when Stottlemyre noticed some of Gooden's best fastballs.

"I said to him, 'Why don't you throw like that all the time?'" Stottlemyre said. "Dwight actually wanted to try it a few years ago because it felt so comfortable, but he never could bring himself to actually change his delivery on the mound."

There was no need to, not when he was toying with National League hitters year after year. But that was then; this was the ugly reality in 1996, when Doc wasn't just out of the rotation but pitching himself out of the organization—and very possibly out of baseball. So on Saturday afternoon, April 20, hours before the Yankees would face the Twins, Stottlemyre and Gooden were alone in the Metrodome's bull pen.

"Doc, I want you try something," the pitching coach said. "First, I want you to get the ball out of your glove a lot quicker, and I want you to make your first step back from the rubber shorter and to the side."

The idea, as Stottlemyre was to explain later to reporters, was to get Gooden's arm and body ready to deliver the ball much quicker than he had with the old windups. As those hurry-up warm-ups at Shea had proved years earlier, Gooden was at his best without the excesses in his delivery. Gooden tried the no-frills windup, and, although it felt strange, he could immediately discern its benefits. The two men worked for twenty minutes, and, that night in his hotel room, Gooden stood in front of the mirror, practicing his delivery.

"It was the first time I'd done anything like that since I was in Little League," Doc said. "My father used to teach that, that the best way to work on your mechanics was to practice in front of the mirror. That's how excited I was. I really thought I'd figured it out."

There was only one problem: how to get into a game. That night at the ballpark, Torre formally announced that Gooden was being dispatched to the bull pen, and he made it clear the fallen right-hander wouldn't be appearing in any close contests.

"I want Dwight to come into a situation where he doesn't feel like he has to make a perfect pitch," Torre said. In other words, Gooden was now the tenth pitcher on the staff, no longer trusted with the pressure of winning or losing. Despite Stottlemyre's advice, and the benefit it might have had in Gooden's sideline workouts, there didn't seem to be anything standing in the way of a release by the Yankees—at least not until six days later.

By then, the Yankees were back in the Bronx and Gooden's day-to-day routine consisted of playing catch in the outfield during batting practice, chatting with reporters, then becoming a spectator to another game. Negron, Gooden's adviser, had been pleading with Doc to remain patient, but there was no consoling the Doctor. "This is what I worked for all these months?" he said, wondering out loud if he and Negron should have accepted the Marlins' final offer.

Doc's frustration became so pointed, he accused Negron of deliberately not responding to the Marlins' last offer until after he'd said yes to the Yankees. Gooden wondered if Negron had used him to gain entry into the Yankee community and thereby land a job as a Steinbrenner consultant.

Negron was shocked by the accusation since, for the last eighteen months, Gooden's recovery had consumed his life too. How many times had Negron been on the phone with Gooden in the fall of '94, talking him through another bad day? How many days had Negron gotten out of bed at 7 A.M. to make sure Gooden went through another workout at Eckerd College in St. Petersburg, then driven with him to the clinic to make sure he took his drug test?

All of this was for free, too, because Negron never asked for a penny. When it came time to sift through the offers, Negron said, "I only told Dwight I thought the Yankees had the best chance for him to restart his career. They were the ones who had the greatest commitment to winning."

Now his client was in trouble, fighting with his agent, fighting his own self-doubts. Who knows how far Gooden would have sunk had Stottlemyre not stopped by his locker that Friday afternoon and asked, "Doc, you feel like starting a game?"

Gooden laughed sadly. "Yeah, where? In Columbus?"

"No, I'm serious," Stottlemyre said. "Coney's gotta take some tests on his hand, and he's gonna have to miss a start tomorrow against the Twins. Joe says it's yours if you want it."

Suddenly, Gooden's heart went off on a sprint again. There it was—a chance, very possibly his last chance. Doc took less than a second to answer the pitching coach.

"Tell Joe I'll be ready," Gooden said. Of course, the Yankees were asking a lot of Doc since it would be his second start in less than a week against the same team that had just beaten him up. Even successful pitchers hate to make back-to-back appearances against the same lineup because, with the increasing familiarity, a pitcher loses the element of surprise.

But the Twins had no idea of the added weapon in Gooden's arsenal. Instead of that confused, long-limbed delivery, Gooden was compact, impossible to time, and throwing fastballs that took even Minnesota's best hitters, Chuck Knoblauch and Paul Molitor, by surprise. In all, Gooden fired six strong innings against Minnesota, allowing just one run on five hits, striking out seven.

Molitor conceded, "That was a different Gooden out there. I don't know what he did, but he was throwing a lot, lot harder, and he seemed to have more confidence."

As much as Gooden tried to pass off the success as "one good start" with "a lot of work ahead of me," he was privately ecstatic at the results. After the game, he said, "That was the best I've felt in so long . . . I'd forgotten what it felt like to be out there dealing, to be in control of the hitters. I love it."

In his next two starts, Gooden was even better, shutting out the White Sox for six innings, then retiring twenty-two Tigers in a row en route to his first victory since 1994. Gooden's resurrection came just in time, too, because doctors had found an aneurysm in Cone's right shoulder, jeopardizing not only his season but also very possibly his career.

By now, Torre was comfortable enough with Gooden's rebuilt fastball to say, "We really need Doc to come through for us in this period." Gooden seemed to love the added responsibility and had patched up his disagreement with Negron. In fact, everything about Gooden's demeanor suggested he was healthy: the hitters were swinging through his fastball, which, thanks to Stottlemyre, had that last-second life again. And there were fewer and fewer bad days, when the urge for cocaine would start to rumble.

Part of the reason was Gooden's friendship with teammate Steve Howe, who, as a recovering addict, understood the war that raged within Gooden's soul. Still hyperactive, and a chain-smoker, Howe was nevertheless in control of his addiction, having remained clean for nearly seven years.

"It really takes three years for an addict to get a leg up on the thing. That's when the urges start to go away," Howe said. "Until then, you have to go to meetings every day, pay attention to it—every fucking day. You gotta respect the addiction. You can never, ever think you've got it beat, or that you can control it. You can't. Man, you gotta be ready to fight it every fucking day of your life."

Such plain talk appealed to Gooden, and many times on the road he and Howe would go to lunch and talk about just that—drugs and how they had changed and nearly ruined their lives. Howe, once a young Dodger fireballer, was now a pariah among the game's conservatives, having relapsed seven times. Howe still couldn't be brought into a game in the Bronx without being booed loudly. And while Howe swore he was deaf to the verbal abuse, he told Gooden one day in April, "It's never going to change for me here. They're running me out of town. Don't let it happen to you. You have a chance to win over the fans."

Howe was right: the fans were enormously tolerant of Gooden's history with drugs, the same demon Howe was fighting. The difference was, Gooden was pitching well and seemed to be a one-man bridge to the postseason, at least as long as Cone was on the disabled list. All Doc had to do was stay clean and keep pitching well and that 1994 relapse would be forgotten in New York.

It seemed like the road to recovery was clear and unfettered until Monday, May 13, when Gooden received a phone call from his sister, Betty, in St. Petersburg. Their father, Dan, who already suffered from failed kidneys that required daily dialysis, was now in need of double-bypass surgery at St. Joseph's Hospital in Tampa. Doctors advised Gooden to be on the first plane to Florida and told the pitcher to prepare for the worst.

Gooden came to the ballpark still in a daze so obvious that Stottlemyre asked, "You okay, Doc?" Gooden shook his head and explained that his father was seriously ill. The two men went directly to Torre's office, where the manager listened briefly to Gooden's assessment of his father's health.

"Look, if you need to get home, go right now," Torre said. "Forget about the game, go be with your father."

Gooden was touched by the manager's gesture but, after considering for a moment, decided against it. He still remembered his father's advice back in 1986, when he was laid up in a New York hospital awaiting hip-replacement surgery.

"He was just about ready for the operation, and because of his kidney problems, the doctors weren't sure how things were going to turn out," Gooden said. "But my dad told me, 'Whatever you're thinking about, I want you to think about pitching and winning. That's what I raised you to be, a baseball player. That's what I want you to do now—pitch.' "

With that memory still so fresh, Gooden decided to remain in New York, pitch against the Mariners on Tuesday, and then take the first plane Wednesday morning to Tampa. Torre asked one last time, "Are you sure, Dwight? Don't do this for me. I'm giving you the option." Gooden thanked Torre but said he was quite sure. He was going to pitch.

All day on Tuesday, Gooden was on the phone with family members, getting up-to-the-minute reports on his father's condition. Doctors were planning to operate the next day; they couldn't wait any longer, and when he finally arrived at the ballpark, Gooden pulled a reporter aside and said, "Whatever happens tonight, I'm dedicating this game to my dad. I want you to write that. This one is for him."

Warming up in the bull pen, Gooden appeared nervous and distracted to Stottlemyre, yet he still seemed to have an exceptionally live fastball. The modified windup was paying a terrific dividend now. All Doc had to do was stay focused.

As Gooden took his eight warm-ups on the mound, Joe Girardi noticed the life in his fastball, too, but he was just as startled by the late, mean break on his slider. As Girardi would say later, "I had the feeling early on that Dwight could throw any of his pitches for strikes at any time, and that's what it takes to throw a no-hitter." Still, there was turbulence early on. Gooden walked Seattle leadoff hitter Darren Bragg on a 3-2 curveball that was just off the plate. That brought the dangerous Alex Rodriguez to the plate—the young shortstop who not only had power and a lightning-quick bat but also the luxury of being protected by Ken Griffey behind him in the lineup.

Although Gooden hadn't been with the Yankees the previous October, he'd seen on TV what Griffey had done to David Cone in game five, hitting a one-out home run in the eighth inning that spelled the beginning of the end for the Yankees.

So the last thing Gooden wanted was to have to pitch to Griffey with both Bragg and Rodriguez on base, which meant he would have to deal with the shortstop head-on. Gooden threw a 1-1 fastball that was supposed to run over the inside corner and prevent Rodriguez from getting the sweet spot of the bat on it. But the pitch had too much of the plate, and, as he had done so many times, Rodriguez took full advantage of the mistake.

He blasted a line drive to right-center, where Gerald Williams was immediately handcuffed. He turned, tracked the ball that was initially sailing to his left, but panicked when he realized Rodriguez's line drive had changed directions and was tailing over his head, toward his right.

"At that point, all I could do was turn, run to a spot, and then just pray I could pick up the ball again," Williams said. "It was a very, very difficult play." He caught the ball with a full-extension stretch, and, even then, there was plenty of white peeking from his glove. Still, Williams was able to deliver a strike to the infield in time to double up Bragg. The crowd went wild, perhaps sensing that this was the start of something very special at the stadium.

They watched as Gooden turned the innings into a blur, as his fastball gained more and more confidence. The Mariners, one of the American League's best-hitting teams, were no match for Gooden, although Doc swore he didn't confront his no-hitter until the seventh inning, when, he recalled, "I came off the field and I saw the fans were going kind of crazy." By then, the Yankees had a 2–0 lead on former teammate Sterling Hitchcock thanks to Tino Martinez's sacrifice fly and Jim Leyritz's RBI single in the sixth. Gooden might have said the seventh was his crossroads, but it actually came in the top of the sixth.

That's when Bragg led off with a sharp bouncer off Martinez's chest. The ball ricocheted into the stands behind first, putting Bragg on second base. The crowd went quiet for a minute as official scorer Bill Shannon digested the play on the press box's TV monitor.

It didn't take Shannon long to rule it an error because, as he put it, "No matter how hard the ball was hit, it was still a three-bouncer off the first baseman's chest." Within moments, the scoreboard relayed the news, changing the Yankees' error total from zero to one. The crowd went wild again, sensing that Gooden was now flirting with history.

Still, Doc had a crisis on his hands: Rodriguez's grounder to Robert Eenhoorn put Bragg on third, and now Griffey was at the plate. There was Junior, wiggling his bat just the way he had last October, moments before taking Cone deep in game five. But this time Doc froze Griffey with a 1-1 slider, down and in. And at 3-2, Gooden threw the best fastball of the night, an up-and-away explosion that, incredibly, made Griffey's bat look slow.

The last three innings were almost surreal. Gooden tried taking deep breaths between innings, standing in the runway next to the dugout. Next to him was Kenny Rogers—who once threw a perfect game as a Ranger—telling him, "Do this for your dad, Dwight. Lock in. Focus, man."

Magically, Gooden found himself in the ninth, the decibel level almost punishing his ears. He walked two in the inning and, thanks to a wild pitch, had runners on second and third and one out, Jay Buhner at the plate.

Gooden knew he was near empty. "Totally out of gas, no legs at all," he remembered. Yet as Torre would later say, "It was Dwight's game, all the way." One last time, Gooden re-loaded the rifle. First, Doc blew away Buhner with a 2-2 fast-ball, up and away and crazy with anger. And then, Paul Sorrento lifted a monstrous pop-up to short, failing, just like all the Mariners, to get a good cut at that monstrous curve-ball.

Even before the ball started its descent, Gooden had raised his fists. Derek Jeter waited and waited, saying later, "I wanted the ball hit to me, even though if I dropped it, my career in New York would've been over."

It took an eternity to end in Jeter's glove, but when it did, when Gooden found himself mobbed by the Yankees on the mound, his eyes became moist. He was carried off the field by his teammates and told reporters, his voice hoarse with ex-haustion, "I never, ever thought I could do this, not in my wildest dreams. It's the best thing that ever happened to me."

In the clubhouse, Gooden immediately telephoned relatives in Florida and learned that his father was still stable, awaiting the bypass surgery.

"Tell Dad I did this for him," Gooden quietly told his sister, Betty.

"You just get down here and tell him yourself," she said.

The next morning, Gooden was on a plane to Tampa, and, as the 727 left LaGuardia, Dan Gooden was undergoing surgery. Doctors worked for four hours to repair the damaged heart and successfully kept the elder Gooden alive. Dwight was at St. Joseph's Hospital the moment his father became conscious, although with tubes everywhere in his body, and still groggy from anesthesia, Dan Gooden couldn't speak.

The pitcher leaned toward his father's ear and said, "I love you, Dad."

Tears flowed down Dan Gooden's cheeks. Doc held his father's hand and started to cry.

6

The Straw That Stirs the Drink

The telephone rang four times, and just like so many times before, an answering machine intercepted Dwight Gooden's call. The voice on the tape sounded distant and uncomfortable:

"No one's in to take your call right now . . . so leave a message."

Gooden paused for a moment, wondering if it was pointless to keep calling his old friend. How many times had Doc already left a message at Darryl Strawberry's home? Six? Eight? Each time, Gooden made sure to leave his St. Petersburg number, even though there wasn't any doubt Strawberry had it.

Obviously, there was a reason why Darryl wasn't returning Doc's calls. But what was it? "The only thing I can think of is that things aren't going too good for him," Doc told a reporter one day in early March. "Shame, man. It ain't right what they're doing to Straw. He'll call me when things get better."

Darryl Strawberry

Of course, Strawberry had gotten the messages, not just from Gooden but also from Gerald Williams, with whom he'd forged a close friendship the previous season in the Bronx. But Williams wasn't getting any return calls, either, at least not during spring training. That's when Strawberry was home in Rancho Mirage, California, looking for a job, waiting for a phone call that never came.

It had been a particularly bad off season for Darryl. His relationship with the Yankees had deteriorated immediately after the play-off loss to the Mariners, when both Buck Showalter and Gene Michael were deposed in an organizational coup. Without either Buck or Stick to act as his advocate, Strawberry was left unprotected in Bob Watson and Joe Torre's redesigned agenda.

Torre had no history or relationship with Darryl, and Watson saw no advantage in signing him. The previous summer, when he was still the general manager of the Astros, Watson had told Bill Goodstein he had "no interest whatsoever" in Strawberry and then promptly hung up on the agent.

Strawberry had played reasonably well with the Yankees in 1995, although with only eighty-seven at-bats, many baseball executives were still unsure whether he could still play a full season and stay healthy—or if his bat speed was still intact. The Yankees still held the option on Strawberry for 1996 at $1.8 million, but Steinbrenner never had any intention of paying Darryl that much. And, in retrospect, Straw had no chance to start the '96 season as a Yankee. Steinbrenner allowed Watson to convince him that Strawberry was a defensive liability and no longer posed the same long-ball threat as he had in the eighties.

Even after Strawberry took a crash course in left field during the Yankees' minicamp in November, the Yankees weren't impressed. They asked him to go to Puerto Rico, where he hit six home runs in his first nine games. Still nothing. On December 3, the Yankees officially told Strawberry he was no longer needed. Furious with Watson, and convinced his career was over, Strawberry angrily boarded a plane, left Puerto Rico, and returned home to Rancho Mirage.

Goodstein begged Darryl to keep playing winter ball, but the agent learned what Darryl's family, friends, and teammates had known for so many years: there was no reasoning with Strawberry when he was angry. Goodstein spent the next month trying to find his client work but was fast discovering the baseball community was still wary of Darryl's demons. In mid-January, Goodstein died of a heart attack in his Manhattan office, and a month later, Strawberry's mother, Ruby, died of cancer.

Strawberry was so lost, so confused, he was on the verge of retirement, ready, as he put it, "to start a life with my church and just forget about baseball." It wasn't that easy, though, since Strawberry still owed the IRS $100,000 in back taxes and was being pressed by his ex-wife, Lisa, for nearly $300,000 in child support.

The antipathy between Strawberry and his former spouse was intense; she was pushing criminal charges and wanted Darryl in jail. With the Yankees out of the picture, and no other teams calling, Strawberry seemed out of options. In fact, when Goodstein died, Strawberry's horizon was so bleak he called a reporter and asked him to get in touch with Red Sox general manager Dan Duquette, who had dropped hints to Goodstein that there might be a home for Strawberry in Boston.

"See what he says," Strawberry told the newsman. "Tell them it's not about money, that all I'm looking for is another chance. Tell them I wasn't any problem for the Yankees."

At least Strawberry had one strong endorsement on his résumé: Buck Showalter himself. Several times the former Yankee manager said, "If anyone wants to know how easy it was to have Darryl in my clubhouse, all they have to do is pick up the phone and call me. He was a professional, came ready to play, and never complained when I sat him. I really don't understand why no one's giving him a chance."

Certainly Strawberry could have played for Showalter's new team, the Arizona Diamondbacks, but they wouldn't begin competition until the 1998 season. By then Strawberry would be going on thirty-six and most likely finished with his career. No, what he needed was someone to take a chance on him immediately.

Duquette? The idea intrigued him, especially since Strawberry's presence would add even more firepower to a lineup that boasted Jose Canseco, Mo Vaughn, and John Valentin. When Strawberry's message was relayed to Duquette, the general manager seemed interested—indeed, he wanted to arrange a breakfast meeting with Darryl during the winter meetings in Los Angeles. But that was the same week that Strawberry flew to New York for Goodstein's funeral, and the two never met face to face.

Soon, Duquette discovered Strawberry was a political time bomb in Boston. The *Boston Herald* mounted a strong campaign against Darryl, and the anti-Strawberry sentiment struck a chord with Sox fans. Was it because of his history with drugs? His tax problems and felony conviction? Domestic violence? Or even that Strawberry was part of the 1986 Met team that devastated all of New England?

Whatever the reason, Duquette wasn't able to sell Strawberry's candidacy to owner John Harrington, who was intimidated by the public backlash. How ironic, then, that Duquette would eventually be allowed to sign Kevin Mitchell, who had a history with the San Diego street gangs in his youth. And even after Mitchell blossomed into a major-league star, he further tarnished his reputation in 1995 by leaving his Japanese team, the Chunichi Dragons, in the middle of the summer with a questionable knee injury.

The difference between Mitchell and Strawberry was perception. No matter how hard he tried to soften his image, Strawberry would always be seen as the bad guy. The same phenomenon occurred with Gooden. It didn't matter that Doc had a much deeper addiction problem than Strawberry. When the conversation turned to second chances, it was Strawberry and Steve Howe who were the examples of baseball's overindulgence.

But Howe had a job with the Yankees. Strawberry did not. As spring training dragged on, he discovered that no one had paid attention to his 1995 resurrection with the Yankees. Or, that if someone had, it wasn't really thought that Strawberry was beyond the long tentacles of his own history.

One American League executive said, "Even if I thought Strawberry could still hit, why should I take a chance that he won't slip up again? Or that some IRS agent isn't going to show up in the dugout right in the middle of a game? Believe me, I don't need that headache."

All Strawberry could do was sit home, stay in shape, and hope for the best. He'd begun searching for a new agent, mulling over suggestions that he seek out Baltimore-based Ron Shapiro or perhaps Dennis Gilbert, the powerful L.A.-based agent who represented, among others, Barry Bonds and Bobby Bonilla.

What Strawberry needed was a high-profile agent who had the influence to pick up the phone and ask a general manager for a favor—at the very least, to get Strawberry an audition in spring training. Interestingly, Strawberry passed over both Shapiro and Gilbert and instead committed himself to Eric

Grossman, Goodstein's son-in-law, a New York attorney who had no prior experience in baseball matters.

Strawberry based this decision purely on loyalty to the Goodstein family. "Bill was there for me when no one wanted to help," Darryl said. "So I'm not going to turn my back on them now. Eric's my guy, and I'm staying with him."

Grossman, with the help of another family friend, Mike Mitchell, also an attorney, called every team in baseball. One by one, the rejections came, except for the Red Sox, who kept the door open just a crack by not actually saying no, but without ever saying yes, either. Grossman grew so frustrated that he finally sent a fax to Duquette indicating Strawberry was willing to travel to spring training at his own expense and pay for his own housing, just for the chance to take batting practice in public.

If the Sox didn't like what they saw, they could release Strawberry without any further contractual obligation. "What we were doing, in essence, was giving teams a free look at Darryl with no strings attached," Grossman said. "And still, no one bit."

It sure had the look and feel of a blacklist. Not even a free tryout for a fit, thirty-four-year-old professional, with nearly three hundred career home runs? The picture became so bleak that even the press's heaviest hitters, Mike Lupica of the New York *Daily News* and Peter Gammons of *The Boston Globe* and ESPN, went out of their way to present Strawberry in a favorable light.

"I think it's time for Darryl to get a job," Lupica told friends in March. "He needs someone to help him out. It's wrong what's happening to him."

But this time, not even Lupica and Gammons's combined might could crack the owners' resolve to keep Strawberry out of the game. Just as in the previous summer, it seemed as if Straw's only hope was for Steinbrenner to change his mind. But several times during spring training, The Boss quashed any possibility of a pardon.

"He broke his promise to us. We wanted him to play left field in Puerto Rico, and he didn't," Steinbrenner said. Eyebrows arched everywhere. Strawberry didn't make out the lineup for the Santurce team; like any player, he did as he was told, playing a little bit of left field, filling in as the designated hitter, and certainly hitting well enough to warrant another season in the Bronx.

The Yankees had a respectable collection of contact hitters who would occasionally hit for power—for instance, Paul O'Neill, Tino Martinez, Ruben Sierra, and Bernie Williams— but there wasn't a single bona fide home run hitter, a guy who could hit the ball to the planets.

There wasn't a single Yankee who could put on the type of batting-practice displays that Strawberry had in Seattle's Kingdome during the 1995 play-offs. With one swing after another, Strawberry would reach the upper deck, sometimes going five hundred feet to right-center. All activity stopped when Darryl walked to the plate. Even the Mariners—including Ken Griffey, Jr.—would freeze the moment Strawberry started to flex his muscles.

Now it seemed the only stage for Strawberry's skills would be at the semiprofessional level. In the final days of spring training, the Red Sox signed Mitchell, ending their courtship with Strawberry, although Duquette had the professional courtesy to respond to Grossman's phone calls. The next question for Strawberry was: What next?

He could retire, of course, and accept baseball's banishment. Strawberry considered Japan, but, as he was to soon find out, that wasn't an option, not with his felony conviction. Strawberry could have found a team in the Mexican League, but that was hardly a choice. With its dingy stadiums and twelve-hour bus rides, Strawberry not only felt that Mexico was beneath him but that his surgically repaired back would suffer, too, sitting up all night in old buses traveling over poorly maintained roads.

The other possibility was the Northern League, a collection of twelve teams scattered throughout the Midwest. Of the seven independent leagues that had sprouted up in recent years, the Northern League was the best. Even though the talent level was somewhere between Class A and Class AA, there were enough former major leaguers to give the league plenty of exposure and enough credibility to be profitable in its first year in 1993.

Founded by *Baseball America* publisher Miles Wolf, the Northern League was supposed to provide fans—and players—an alternative to the traditional minor-league farm system. There was a refreshing honesty about the league's credo: the owners invested money to make money, not to develop talent, and the players used the Northern League as a springboard to the majors.

It was a long shot, though. For the most part, the rosters were full of minor-league rejects or former major leaguers trying to resurrect careers that had seen their best days. Leon Durham, the Cubs' ex–first baseman, was still toiling in the Northern League, as was right-hander Jack Morris, who only five years earlier with the Twins had thrown ten shutout innings in game seven of the World Series to beat the Atlanta Braves.

Grossman made some telephone calls on Strawberry's behalf and found there'd be room for him on the St. Paul Saints. The Saints were owned by Marvin Goldklang, a limited partner in the Yankee hierarchy, and Grossman properly reasoned that if Strawberry played well and treated his teammates and fans well, the Yankees sooner or later would come around.

Trouble was, Strawberry wasn't interested. "Why should I play there?" he asked a reporter over the phone. It sure wouldn't be for the money. The Northern League would only pay $2,500 a month, which would barely coat the linings of his debt to the Internal Revenue Service and to his former wife.

But Grossman, as well as Strawberry's friends, tried to make Darryl understand that this was his last chance. And what better way for Straw to state his case than hit one five-hundred-foot home run after another in front of all the TV cameras that would surely follow him around? Grossman even petitioned members of the media who were close to Strawberry to ask him to reconsider instead of remaining at home, playing the victim.

The Yankees, meanwhile, hardly even mentioned Strawberry's name. Torre simply said he had never managed Darryl and didn't know whether he could help. And Watson asked, "Where am I supposed to play him? Where does Darryl Strawberry fit on this team?"

It didn't take any great deductive power to determine the Strawberry-Yankee divorce was now complete. In the last days of spring training, when someone asked Watson if, in any way, he had been thinking of Strawberry, the general manager smiled the smuggest of smiles.

"Strawberry?" Watson said. "Oh, sure I've thought of strawberry. Had strawberry shortcake for dessert last night. It was good too."

It had been five months since Dwight Gooden had signed with the Yankees, and not once had he been in trouble. It wasn't just the steady stream of negative drug tests that pleased Steinbrenner but the fact that Gooden had never been late to the clubhouse, never complained to reporters when he was taken out of the rotation, and, above all, was good to the fans.

That meant a lot to Steinbrenner, who was still reeling from the public relations disaster that followed Strawberry's signing in 1995. The Boss thought he would be perceived as a savior—as the father figure who finally defeated Darryl's demons—only to hear criticism all the way from the White House. In fact, Strawberry's tenure with the Yankees was doomed the day President Clinton's drug czar, Lee Brown, said that by giving Strawberry another chance the Yankees were "sending the wrong message" to America's youth.

The last thing the Yankees needed was for Gooden to suffer a relapse. But Doc's perfect record as a Yankee finally opened the door to Strawberry's return. Having joined the St. Paul Saints, he was destroying Northern League pitchers, hitting in the near .400s, averaging a home run almost every six at-bats. If the league's pitchers were so incompetent, as Strawberry's detractors insisted, then why was he the only one hitting so many homers?

On June 25, Steinbrenner telephoned Ray Negron, who'd been serving both as Gooden's adviser and as a Yankee consultant. The Boss asked Negron, who had teamed with Goodstein early in 1995 in representing Straw, what he knew about Darryl's commitment to sobriety and how he'd handle a return to New York.

"All I can tell you is that being in New York hasn't been a problem for Dwight," Negron said. "He knows what he has to do to stay clean."

And if that were true for Gooden, then it figured Strawberry would behave, too, since Doc's addiction had been so much deeper. Steinbrenner had spoken to Marvin Goldklang several times in the previous week and heard that Darryl had been living a quiet off-the-field life with his second wife and family. Furthermore, Strawberry routinely signed autographs for fans outside the ballpark in St. Paul, patiently handling hundreds of requests every night.

Finally, it seemed, Strawberry had shed the arrogance of his youth. "I'm doing the best I can with my life," Strawberry said. "For a while, after Bill and my mother died, I lost my love of baseball, and I didn't care if I ever put on the uniform again. But playing in the Northern League made me appreciate what baseball is all about. If things don't work and I don't get another chance, at least I'll know I gave it my all this year. That's good enough for me."

Strawberry had delivered similar sales pitches in the past, but this one seemed more genuine. Darryl didn't even seem discouraged when on June 24, with the Yankees playing the Twins only twenty minutes away, Bob Watson refused to make a personal scouting trip to St. Paul.

"We have our normal coverage. I wouldn't want to give anyone the wrong idea by going there myself," Watson said. "What I hear is that not much is new with Darryl: he's hitting okay, but not doing much in the field."

In the next few minutes, Watson told reporters five times that Strawberry "doesn't fit" with the Yankees. Five times. Yet, the front-office machinery was already at work to sign Darryl. There are two theories to explain the discrepancy. Either Watson was completely removed from Steinbrenner's decision-making impulses and was actually speaking honestly with newsmen or else the Yankees were playing rope-a-dope with the Orioles, who were also sniffing around Darryl. By emphatically stating they had no interest in Strawberry, the Yankees might have gotten the O's to relax and perhaps take an extra few days to scout Darryl.

Either way, Steinbrenner shocked the baseball community on July 4 when he signed Darryl to a one-year deal worth $700,000. After proration, Darryl would receive about $350,000 as well as a signing bonus of $260,000, which went directly to Lisa Strawberry. Once again, Steinbrenner had become Darryl's life preserver, providing just enough up-front cash to satisfy the courts. Strawberry was in jeopardy of defaulting on his support payments, and a trial in Los Angeles was set to begin in a matter of days.

No wonder Strawberry was so grateful. He told reporters, "I know I've made a lot of mistakes in my life. But at least I have this one last chance to get it right. At this point I'm grateful for whatever baseball I have left."

Steinbrenner, of course, never referred to the six-month exile he imposed on Darryl or why, if he was willing to forgive and forget in July, that couldn't have been the case in February or April. "All I'll say is that it's time to heal and to move on," Steinbrenner said. "I was impressed with the way Darryl conducted himself in St. Paul and the way he treated fans. He was devoted to his family, and that was important to me."

The real question was whether Strawberry's final Northern League stats would mean much against major-league pitching: a .435 average, eighteen home runs in only 108 at-bats, and thirty-nine RBIs. With Tim Raines on the disabled list, Strawberry not only could serve as the designated hitter, but he might even play some left field.

But it wasn't just Raines who'd get squeezed by Darryl. Ruben Sierra's days would be numbered, too, since he'd hit only nine home runs in 301 at-bats, slumping so badly—and waving so helplessly at pitches out of the strike zone—that it was sometimes embarrassing to watch.

Maybe that's why none of the Yankees seemed to mind Strawberry's addition to the team—least of all Gooden, who said, "It's about time we brought him here." Darryl had already proven himself a year earlier as a model clubhouse citizen—certainly no worse than Steve Howe, whom the club had released two weeks earlier. In fact, the only voice of dissent belonged to Mariano Duncan, Sierra's best friend among the Yankees, who said, bitterly, "It's not like we were in last place or anything."

After a two-game tune-up at Class AAA Columbus—during which he hit three home runs in eight at-bats—Strawberry arrived at the stadium on July 7. He looked leaner than in past years, having backed off his monstrous weight-lifting regimens. He looked gentler in the face, too, humbled by all the years of drugs and drinking and back-page controversy.

One by one, from locker to locker, Strawberry greeted his teammates with a handshake, waiting until the very end to be reunited with an old friend from the eighties.

"Doc, man," Strawberry said, embracing Gooden.

"About time, cuz," Gooden said.

After so many years, Darryl and Dwight were back together. How long had it been since they ruled New York? Since all they had to do was show up at the ballpark, throw a fastball, take a few swings, and the Mets' world was safe?

It had been just five years, and, in one sense, it felt like a millennium. Strawberry and Gooden had both fallen so far, and they were now so grateful for this one last dance with baseball. But the stadium was transformed the moment Strawberry came to the plate in the first inning against the Brewers' Ben McDonald.

Suddenly, the Bronx became Flushing, the nineties rewound to the eighties. There was Strawberry, taking in a standing ovation from the crowd. Darryl had always considered himself a big-moment player, always doing his best work when the adrenaline was running at full blast. And, no doubt, this was one of the biggest moments of his career.

On the very first pitch he saw, Strawberry ripped a line drive to right field that, for a half-second, looked as if it might clear the wall. The crowd rose to its feet, awed by the possibility that Strawberry could return from exile and, in just one swing, recapture his crown as New York's most charismatic player.

Could he? Did he? Not quite. The ball ended in right fielder Matt Mieske's glove at the warning track. It was the most delicious of teases, but the message was clear. Even after going 0-for-4 that day, Strawberry was making the Yankees look smart. And even at 0-for-10, the anticipation kept growing.

It wasn't until the Yankees were in Baltimore on July 13 that Strawberry finally flexed his muscles. Maybe it was all the old faces that brought back the voodoo—seeing Randy Myers and Jesse Orosco and Roger McDowell in the outfield during batting practice and his old manager Davey Johnson in the Orioles dugout while Strawberry hit one batting-practice blast after another.

"He looked at me like, 'Why aren't you here? You should've been here,' " Strawberry said. Privately, Johnson said the Orioles had taken the word of Rick Down, their hitting coach who served in a similar role under Buck Showalter in 1995, who said Strawberry had lost his bat speed. Now it was time for Darryl to make the Orioles pay for their reluctance. In the third inning of the second game of a doubleheader, Strawberry powered a two-run home run off right-hander Rocky Coppinger.

It was a classic Strawberry home run—high and long and arrogant, the kind that crushed the sold-out crowd at Camden Yards. And, just to make his point, Strawberry overpowered Arthur Rhodes in the fifth inning, pummeling another two-run homer into the right-field seats. Strawberry circled the bases in that loose, disjointed trot he used to have at Shea, and, when he returned to the dugout, he was swallowed up in a sea of Yankee high-fives.

Strawberry worked his way through the roster before he finally found Gooden. As it turned out, it wasn't Myers or Orosco or Davey who served as Darryl's catalysts—it was Doc, who was pitching that day. Of course. Just like old times: Doc threw the heaters, Darryl hit the ball to the planets.

The two old Mets smiled when they finally high-fived at the top step of the dugout.

"Way to pick me up, big man," Gooden said.

"Like it used to be, Doc," Strawberry said.

No other words were said. After so many years, none were needed.

7

The Sweeps

The clubhouse was never so solemn after a win. And not just any win, but a doubleheader win that defied all odds. Indeed, in a season of magic moments from marquee names such as Doc and Darryl and Cone and Key, the Yankees performed their most extraordinary trick of all by hitting a daily double with Brian Boehringer and Ramiro Mendoza on the mound in Cleveland.

They started the day-night doubleheader on June 22 just hoping to limit the bloodshed and wound up humbling the mighty American League champion Indians with a sweep in Jacobs Field.

As Dwight Gooden would say at the season's end: "After that day in Cleveland we started thinking, 'Hey, something's going on here.' "

But there was no postgame giddiness. Moments after the final out, the players learned that Joe Torre's brother Rocco

Andy Pettitte

had died of a heart attack in New York after watching the Yankees come back from a 5–1 deficit to win the first game of the doubleheader by an 8–7 score.

In his office Torre was somber as he met the press, doing all he could to hold back tears. Rocco, sixty-nine, was a retired New York police officer and drug enforcement agent who lived in Flushing, Queens. Like the rest of the Torre family, Rocco had grown up in Brooklyn despising the Yankees as they dominated baseball. But all of that changed when his kid brother became their manager.

"He was a Yankee fan now," Torre said that day. "He was a fan of mine."

Torre had received the news between games when his wife, Alice, got a call through to his office. When she asked him if he was sitting down, Torre said he thought immediately of his brother Frank, the former major leaguer who was in a Florida hospital at the time because of heart problems, the brother who would wind up in New York awaiting a heart transplant during the Yankees' championship run.

No, Alice told her husband, it was Rocco.

"It was like someone hit you in the face," Torre said quietly.

His players didn't know at the time that Torre managed the second game with a heavy heart. It was hard for him to enjoy, but certainly he could appreciate the accomplishment as the Yankees completed their sweep, routing the big, bad Indians, 9–3.

"All we were trying to do was hold our own," Torre admitted.

Given the circumstances, the sweep was nearly unfathomable. The Yankees went to Cleveland carrying cold bats, and their pitching was in a tattered state, decimated by injuries.

Melido Perez and Scott Kamieniecki were afterthoughts at this point, buried under the weight of constant elbow problems. David Cone was long gone after his aneurysm surgery. Jimmy Key was on the fifteen-day disabled list for the second time in the space of five weeks, and while it was a calf muscle this time, his postsurgical shoulder was still giving him problems. Most troubling of all, Andy Pettitte was suffering from pain in his elbow that would bother him for weeks.

So it was that they were forced to pitch Boehringer and Mendoza, who had only a handful of major-league starts between them, against the Indians. But what loomed as a slaughter became another showcase for the Yankees' tenacity. All year they would respond offensively just when it seemed they might never get another hit, and on this day they rallied to beat Jose Mesa, the Indians' closer who had been untouchable in 1995, and then they flexed their muscles to pound seventeen hits in the nightcap.

When it was over the Yankees were riding an adrenaline high, juiced by their own accomplishment. But when they learned of Torre's loss, the energy was immediately drained from the room. The players' strong respect for Torre had an immediate sobering effect on their celebration.

By this time they had come to appreciate the combination of Torre's relaxed approach and hard-edged desire to win. They could see he was secure in his ability to manage, unconcerned about the peripheral issues that continually surround the Yankees. He'd made it clear that, as a player who had hit as high as .363 and as low as .247, he understood the often grim nature of grinding through the failure inherent in a baseball season. He was on their side all the way as long as they hustled, concentrated, and understood that he was managing, at age fifty-five, not to win any friends in the clubhouse but to do whatever it took to reach the World Series that had eluded him in more than thirty years of playing and managing in the big leagues. He could be warm and car-ing to a player in need of a lift but as cold as an assassin if necessary.

"Everybody's got their envelope," Torre said one day, speaking of his temper. "I've got no patience for mental mistakes or nonpreparation."

He had a way of putting players in their place when he felt it necessary. There had been a game in which Torre went to the mound to take out a struggling Jeff Nelson, except Nelson was hoping to convince the manager otherwise.

"I can get this guy, Joe," Nelson said of the next hitter. "Let me get this guy."

Torre, who had already signaled for another pitcher, let Nelson know this was no place for a debate.

"Then what the fuck am I here for?" he said evenly, looking Nelson in the eye. "You want to manage?"

Nelson handed him the ball and walked off the mound without a word.

Torre never purposely embarrasses his players publicly, however. He always defends them to the press, but he knows how to make a point. He would sit Paul O'Neill down for two games in July after O'Neill embarrassed himself one day by getting thrown out on a ground ball despite a bad throw because he jogged down the line in frustration. In that case Torre was critical publicly of O'Neill's failure to hustle, but he insisted he only sat him down to help him break out of a slump. His players got the message, though.

"The thing about Joe," David Cone said one day, "is that he doesn't care about the little things. He doesn't worry about the media, and he doesn't worry about George [Steinbrenner], and he doesn't worry about whether a player is mad at him. He's not trying to impress anyone. He just wants to win."

But after the biggest of wins, a doubleheader sweep to remember, there was no joy for Torre. He would take the lineup card from the first game, the last game Rocco saw, and put it in his brother's coffin, along with a Yankee cap, at the wake two days later.

While Torre made plans to attend Rocco's funeral, the Yankees continued their domination of the Indians the next day. And again they showed their toughness with another comeback win. By now their surefire success formula consisted of a starting pitcher getting to the seventh inning with a lead for Mariano Rivera and John Wetteland to protect. But their comebacks were becoming a trait as well: in April they had come back from a 6–1 deficit in Baltimore to defeat the Orioles, 10–7; in May they had come back from an 8–0 deficit in Chicago to nip the White Sox, 9–8; and now, one day after rallying from being down 5–1, they did it again to the Indians, coming back from a 5–0 deficit to win 11–9 largely on the strength of two Ruben Sierra home runs.

"A lot of teams say they can always come back," John Wetteland said that day. "There's a difference when you're able to do it."

Those would be words to remember come October, but they were significant enough already. In addition, another trend was developing: the closer the game, the better the Yankees liked it. A stellar bull pen and a steady defense—only the Texas Rangers would make fewer errors in '96—made them tough to beat at crunch time, and by the season's end nobody would have a better record in one-run games than the Yankees.

Sure enough, with Don Zimmer managing in Torre's absence the following day, the Yankees completed their astonishing four-game sweep of the Indians with a 6–5 win that Gerald Williams saved with a dashing, leaping catch of Kenny Lofton's line drive in left field. The four-game sweep was the Yankees' first in Cleveland since 1964, when one George M.

Steinbrenner III still lived there, and it completed a six-game season sweep at Jacobs Field.

Their superiority over the Indians was unmatched; no other team in the league had a winning record in Jacobs Field, and yet the Yankees were 10-2 there in 1995 and '96. They hoped it would mean something come October, since they assumed any road to the World Series would lead through Cleveland.

As Torre had said after the win a day earlier, "We're not intimidated coming in here."

As uplifting as the sweep was for the Yankees, the events of the next few days in Minneapolis were perhaps even more revealing of their destination. They were so uncertain of Pettitte's elbow pain that they flew in Double A pitcher Mike Buddie from Norwich, Connecticut, to stand by as Pettitte warmed up. Just in case.

Pettitte hadn't pitched in ten days because of the elbow pain, and it did hurt him as he warmed up. But he told Mel Stottlemyre he was okay, then fought through the discomfort to pitch a solid five and a third innings, surrendering two runs while allowing the Bomber brain trust to exhale. A 3–0 loss was actually cause for optimism.

"We've got a pitcher back," said Joe Torre, who arrived during the game after laying his brother to rest in New York that morning. "That's important."

Two days later they had another one back, as Jimmy Key returned from the disabled list to pitch seven strong innings in a 2–1 victory. After a remarkably rapid return from shoulder surgery, Key had been searching throughout the season for the precision that had made him one of the best pitchers in baseball during a twelve-year career.

Over the first three months his ERA had hovered between six and seven, an embarrassment for a pitcher of his stature. Key, a proud man, insisted he would retire if he could not approach his former level of brilliance, but he knew he had to endure a little agony to find out if he still had a career.

"I'm giving myself this season to find out," Key said that night. "If I can't win consistently, I'll walk away. But I'm willing to take some lumps for the chance to be right for this team in September and October."

That determination would eventually pay huge dividends. As it was, this night gave the Yankees reason to believe again as Key painted the corners in his classic style. But that wasn't the only omen. Indeed, the month of June seemed to be full of them. Only a week earlier rain had washed out a 5–1 deficit to the Twins at the stadium, leading the would-be loser, Dwight Gooden, to say, "It's the first time I can remember guys shaking my hand for a rainout."

Now fate seemed to intervene again in the form of a ninth-inning blunder. Twins base runner Pat Meares was poised to score the tying run from third base in the ninth inning on Chuck Knoblauch's fly ball to right, but when third-base coach Scott Ullger shouted, "Go, go go," Meares thought he heard, "No, no, no." He stayed put, and the Yankees said thank you as John Wetteland promptly struck out Jeff Reboulet to secure Key's 2–1 victory.

In another season it may have been nothing more than a good break lost among the ups and downs of 162 games. In this one it had the feel of destiny.

Whatever that destiny was, bad weather clearly seemed to be part of it. They'd been snowed out on Opening Day in Cleveland. They'd played in a winter wonderland in their home opener. Rain would play no small part in their meetings with the Orioles throughout the season, and now as they pulled into Baltimore to open the season's second half, a hurricane was waiting.

Hurricane Bertha, later downgraded to a tropical storm, would wipe out the second game of the series, forcing a Saturday doubleheader. It seemed fitting enough, given the storm clouds that continued to surround the Orioles.

While the Yankees had basked in their first-place glory during the All-Star break, the O's had done some soul-searching, trying to sort out their problems. Their early-season conflicts had escalated into full-blown turmoil in May and June, coming to something of a head two weeks earlier when O's owner Peter Angelos weighed in with his opinion just as the Orioles went to New York for four games in Yankee Stadium.

Angelos suggested to reporters that Cal Ripken should be more of a leader in the clubhouse, that he should be the one to put an end to the bickering and influence his teammates to focus on baseball. Ripken, furious when the story hit the papers, immediately phoned Angelos and hashed it out with him.

The Orioles split that four-game series in New York, but even a 9–1 laugher in the series finale couldn't produce a smile in the visiting clubhouse. Brady Anderson was the latest unhappy Bird, in a snit because Johnson had moved him from leadoff to third in the lineup in an attempt to shake up a lethargic offense. Even David Wells, the winning pitcher on this day and a free spirit, was a miserable soul; upset at media criticism over his mediocre season to date, Wells told the press to take a hike when reporters sidled up to his locker.

Luis Polonia, a free spirit and former Yankee, surveyed the room after the win and said, "It sure is quiet here. It wasn't like this with the Yankees. We enjoyed our wins. This isn't good." Polonia would have stronger words for the Orioles when he was released a few weeks later, saying, "Everybody's out for themselves there."

In the visiting manager's office, meanwhile, Davey Johnson looked like a man who couldn't get rid of a headache. The resistance from his own ballclub was wearing on him. "Every time I want to change something, it can't be a catastrophe," he said that day. "I'm tired of every time I do something, the world shows up to write about it." Davey wasn't mad at the writers, but, short of calling his players a bunch of underachieving whiners, it was the only way to release some frustration.

Now, back from the All-Star break, Johnson called Ripken in for a private meeting and asked for his help in smoothing the clubhouse waters. Ripken agreed to put the problems of the first half behind him, and the Orioles began the long weekend series that Thursday, July 11, against the Yankees with renewed hope that things would be different over the final three months.

Instead, by Sunday the Birds were wondering what had hit them. The Yankees beat them four times, each game in doubt to the end, each one sealed by the bull pen in what amounted to another foreshadowing of October. Yankee relievers pitched a total of ten and a third innings in the series and surrendered not a single run. John Wetteland earned saves in all four games, pitching an inning in each end of the doubleheader.

Suddenly, the bull pen was more than just a weapon. Suddenly, the Yankees had an aura of invincibility. You could hear it in Mike Mussina's voice after the first game of the series, when he gave up an eighth-inning home run to Derek Jeter that turned a 2–2 tie into a 4–2 Yankee win. Mussina chastised himself at his locker that night, saying, "You just can't give them the lead late in the game like that—their bull pen is just too good."

It's an aura that seems to be a requirement for championship teams. In the late eighties Dennis Eckersley gave the Oakland A's the feeling they couldn't lose in the late innings.

The Nasty Boys—Rob Dibble, Norm Charlton, and Randy Myers—did the same for the champion Cincinnati Reds in 1990. The Blue Jays won two straight World Series in the nineties with only adequate starting pitching that was reinforced by the nuclear bull-pen duo of Duane Ward and Tom Henke. Even the Braves, with the best starting staff in baseball, couldn't win it all until Mark Wohlers matured into a reliable closer.

Jimmy Key was a Blue Jay in '92, the first of the back-to-back Toronto championship years. He saw Ward and Henke make the late innings automatic, and now he was seeing Rivera and Wetteland do the same.

"There's a psychological edge," said Key, who earned the win in the first game of the Orioles series. "Teams play with the thought in their mind that they can't be behind you by the sixth or seventh inning. I saw it in Toronto, and it's a similar feeling with our bull pen. Especially when you have power guys down there who can come in and get strikeouts. It does something to the other team, knowing you've got guys who can come in and just take the game right out of their hands."

The bull pen gave the Yankees a huge edge against Baltimore, but the more the two teams played each other, the more it appeared that intangibles were a factor.

It may not be easy to define chemistry, but its impact is undeniable. In this case the Yankees' chemistry was as good as the Orioles' was bad. The difference was never more apparent than in the reactions of the managers after the first game of the Saturday doubleheader.

The Yankees stunned the O's by rallying for two runs in the ninth inning to win, 3–2. Clubhouses are closed between games of a doubleheader, but Torre ushered the press into his office, where he leaned back in a chair, lit up one of his favorite cigars, and enjoyed the moment.

"We didn't have anything going," Torre said. "And to come back the way we did . . ."

Torre didn't try to explain it. No need, the way his team was playing.

Down the hall, meanwhile, Davey Johnson had the look of a government witness taking the stand. He came out into the hallway to meet the press, no doubt so that he could walk away if the grilling became too uncomfortable.

But nobody in Baltimore was after Davey's hide. He had become a sympathetic figure of sorts, a manager at the mercy of cellular-packing, agent-calling, ego-toting players of the nineties. And now he seemed to be utterly baffled by his team's inability to hang tough in the late innings.

"We're just not getting the big out or the big hit against them," Johnson said. "We've got to play with more confidence."

The contrast in attitude, indeed, in the makeup of the two teams, was becoming more and more striking. The Yankees were the definition of professionals. As the season continued Torre would refer to them repeatedly as "throwbacks," a team willing to sacrifice individual ego in the name of winning.

It was a refreshing change for Torre, who became disenchanted with managing when he got caught in the middle of the players' strike in '94 and '95 in St. Louis. Like all major-league managers except Sparky Anderson, Torre agreed to manage replacement players in the spring of '95, and he was startled to find the regular players resented him for it when they returned.

"It really put a sour taste in my mouth," Torre said one day late in the season. "I had always felt I was a players' manager, and to have them react that way toward me . . . I didn't know if I wanted to manage again.

"But this team has been a joy. A lot of players talk about wanting to win these days, but most of them don't really know what it takes. They think if they go out and put the numbers up, that's enough. But you have to do the things to glue those cracks together through the course of a season. It's a feeling, an attitude.

"You have to go beyond that wall of numbers. You have to do the little things that don't show up in the box score. You have to put pressure on the defense by running hard all the time. You can't get caught up in ego. This team understands. They respect the fact that I have decisions to make, and I respect the fact that they're busting their ass."

Whatever the formula, the Yankees were continuing to defy logic. Their ninth-inning rally that beat the Orioles in the first game of the doubleheader was the work of the Murderers' Row of Gerald Williams, Joe Girardi, and Mariano Duncan. And a career minor leaguer named Matt Howard, who would be released before the season's end, had made the runs meaningful with a great diving play at third base the previous inning to cut short an Orioles rally.

Torre wasn't trying to take credit for any of it as the Yankees rolled along, but so much of their success seemed to come back to his cool, calm, confident handling of the ball club.

Not to mention his honesty. On this day, for example, Torre was asked to explain why, after pinch-hitting for Howard in the ninth, he inserted rookie Andy Fox at third base rather than his two-time Gold Glove, Wade Boggs.

"The kid is better defensively," Torre said matter-of-factly.

Sensing the raised antennae of reporters accustomed to code-word answers from managers, Torre explained further: "Wade's very good defensively, but the kid is younger. He has young legs—more range to both sides."

It was the rarest of answers by a big-league manager because while it was not meant as such, it could have been construed as an insult to Boggs. Yet Torre didn't give it a second thought, and by this point of the season it was clear the Yankees had embraced his straightforward style, putting the ball club ahead of the selfishness that was dragging down the Orioles.

Come the nightcap, it was the Birds who desperately needed to be energized. Instead, the Yankees unleashed their newest weapon as Darryl Strawberry hit a pair of home runs to further demoralize the Orioles in a 7–5 victory that completed the doubleheader sweep.

By Sunday the sweep of the series was inevitable. The weekend had become all too humiliating for the home team, and not only because of the games themselves. So many Yankee fans had made the drive down I-95 and found tickets that the O's could have sworn they were playing in the Bronx. The Yankee cheering was such that on Sunday a columnist for the Baltimore *Sun* chided Orioles fans for selling their tickets—the games were all sellouts—to New Yorkers and urged them to make a stand for the series finale.

It turned out that Custer made a better stand, as the Yanks finished off the sweep with a 4–1 victory and Camden Yards rocked with chants of "Let's go, Yankees." At the day's end the Orioles were ten games behind the Yankees, and a dazed Davey Johnson was saying it was time to make changes with his team.

The Yankees, meanwhile, quietly celebrated their feat. In the space of three weeks they had swept the two teams that had loomed as American League favorites when the season began, swept them in enemy territory. It was a heady accomplishment, and while it wasn't their style to talk as big as they played, the Yankees left town thinking they'd buried the Orioles for good.

8

Low Tide Coming

E ven from the dugout, the Yankees could see that Ruben Sierra was standing too far away from the plate, unable to cover the outer regions of the strike zone. Over and over, Joe Torre had tried to explain to Sierra that American League pitchers had found a flaw in his swing and were going to exploit it until he moved closer to the plate and started hitting the outside-corner strike to the opposite field.

Trouble was, it was already late July and Sierra still didn't get the message. The days went by in a steady blur and Sierra was still trying to pull everything, trying to reach the planets with his home runs. Sierra behaved as if it were still 1989 and he was a younger, leaner Texas Ranger, with the bat speed to hit twenty-nine home runs and lead the American League with 119 RBIs. Sierra was only twenty-three then and had all the credentials to become one of the game's premier power hitters.

John Wetteland

But here he was as a Yankee seven years later—slower, heavier, and far more stubborn. Sierra had developed a huge front leg kick as he began his weight shift. That, in itself, wouldn't have been such a detriment had he also not fallen into the habit of stepping away from pitches as he swung. As a result, Sierra was swinging entirely with his arms, waving pathetically at the ball. All a smart pitcher had to do was place a fastball six inches off the outside corner and Sierra was history.

Joe Torre had no idea what to do with his troubled outfielder/designated hitter, since Darryl Strawberry looked as if he had the bat speed to help the Yankees, and, sooner or later, Tim Raines would return from the disabled list. It didn't help Sierra's cause, either, that he'd alienated Torre six weeks earlier, when he was briefly benched.

Insisting that Torre had promised him the everyday job in left field, Sierra flatly called Torre a "liar." There it was: the first evidence that Sierra was about to become a clubhouse cancer. The A's, who had traded Sierra to the Yankees in July of 1995 in exchange for Danny Tartabull, had guaranteed that, sooner or later, Sierra would live up to Tony LaRussa's label of "village idiot."

"Just watch. He's one of the biggest jerks in baseball," said one Oakland executive. Now Sierra's indictment of Torre was splattered all over the back pages of the *Post* and *Daily News,* and while the manager handled the crisis with remarkable calm, none of the Yankees—neither the front office nor the players—ever took Sierra seriously again.

In fact, one American League executive said the Yankees were telling outsiders that Sierra was nothing more than "a lightweight" who would have to be sent elsewhere. Finally, as the trading deadline approached, that prophecy was fulfilled.

When the message on Bob Watson's desk said Tigers general manager Randy Smith had called, the Yankee general manager knew exactly what was about to unfold. Several months earlier, as far back as spring training, Watson had asked the Tigers about Cecil Fielder, the monstrous, larger-than-life—if not slightly larger-than-his-uniform—designated hitter.

Watson knew the Yankees needed right-handed power, and it was too much to ask Bernie Williams to accept that entire responsibility, especially since, as a switch hitter, he only batted from the right side against left-handed pitching. As for Sierra . . . well, he had only eleven home runs in 360 at-bats, and the Yankees were only 15-16 against left-handed pitching.

The Yankees were convinced they'd have to face the Mariners again in the play-offs, and the thought of left-handed pitchers dominating the lineup—including Randy Johnson and his fastball, along with Sterling Hitchcock, the former Yankee who'd been pitching so well in Seattle, and Norm Charlton—was all too much for Watson to tolerate.

So Watson knew it was time to make a dramatic move—getting Fielder, giving the Yankees the same home run quotient from the right side that Strawberry provided from the left. The Tigers were desperate to acquire good young pitching with which to rebuild, so in order to obtain Yankee prospect Matt Drews, they agreed to take on Sierra, somehow hoping that he'd regain his equilibrium in a low-pressure, zero-anxiety setting.

The Tigers knew that Fielder was enormously popular with their fans. In fact, he and shortstop Alan Trammell were the only goodwill ambassadors the club had as it underwent a massive rebuilding campaign. Day in and day out, "Big Daddy," as he was affectionately known around the league, showed up for work and hit home runs for a team going nowhere. Finally, Smith decided to reward his best player, knowing that, at age thirty-two, Fielder wouldn't be around to reap the benefits of the Tigers' long-term restructuring.

On July 31, the in-season trading deadline, Smith approached Fielder after the Tigers had lost another ball game and said, "Big Daddy, I'm sending you to a good place, the Yankees. Go win a pennant, big man. Go get it done."

Fielder beamed, extended his hand to Smith, and said, simply, "Thank you, Randy. This is what I've been waiting for for a long time."

Halfway across the country, the reaction was far more severe. The Yankees had just lost their second straight game to the Rangers. Although the Yankees were ten games ahead of the Orioles, the Bombers' vulnerability against left-handers was becoming more apparent. Texas southpaw Darren Oliver scattered nine hits in seven innings as the Yankees went down, 9–2. In two nights in Arlington, the Yankees had been outscored 24–4, and Sierra was a combined 2-for-8 with just two infield singles.

In a thinly veiled indictment of his left fielder, Watson said, "We're just not getting enough production from the right side." After the game, third-base coach Willie Randolph told Sierra that Torre wanted to see him in his office. Without a word, Sierra walked in, and Torre told him to close the door.

"Ruben, we're making a move with the Tigers," Torre said. "We've traded you to Detroit for Fielder."

Torre paused a moment, waiting for a reaction from Sierra. There was none. Torre then handed him a slip of paper.

"Here's Randy Smith's number. He'll help you make the arrangements."

Torre waited another moment, the silence filling the room. When it became clear the manager had nothing else to say, Sierra simply turned around and walked out the door. In the clubhouse, he dressed quickly, not bothering to say good-bye to anyone except Mariano Duncan, not even pausing to gather his belongings.

"He's very, very upset," Duncan told reporters a few minutes later. "I think Ruben just wants to go back to the hotel and relax and think about things first."

Weeks later, when the Tigers visited New York, Sierra blasted his former teammates, claiming, "No one showed me any respect. No one even said good-bye." Even Duncan refuted Sierra's recollection, saying, "The reason no one said good-bye is because Ruben left before anyone had a chance. I'm sorry he felt that way."

The truth was, no one really cared that Sierra was leaving town, taking with him his strange, unrelenting moodiness, his silence, and the belief that all he needed to get out of his slump was to keep playing. Sierra was being sent to his personal nirvana, where he would be guaranteed four at-bats a day, regardless of how poorly he hit, regardless of how many games the Tigers lost.

As for Fielder, the Yankees were ecstatic. As Dwight Gooden put it, "If he can hit that many home runs for a bad team, imagine what he can do in this lineup. It's an awesome trade."

By including minor-league right-hander Matt Drews in the deal, the Yankees also officially gave up on their number-one pick in the 1993 draft. Drews had struggled on all three levels of the club's farm in 1996, posting a combined record of 1-10 with a 6.00 ERA. Drews, twenty-one, had most recently been pitching at Class AA Norwich.

Even after acquiring Fielder, the Yankees weren't done dealing. With just fifteen minutes left before the midnight trading deadline was to expire, Watson sent right-hander Mark Hutton to the Florida Marlins in exchange for another righty, David Weathers. That swap had far less impact than Fielder's acquisition, but it showed how little spring-training rhetoric can mean in the regular season.

Every day in March, the Yankees had trumpeted their praise of Hutton, the hulking 6'6" Australian who had once played Australian-rules football. Given his size and a ninety-plus sinker, Watson and Torre considered him untouchable. But that was before Hutton suffered the third torn groin muscle of his four-year career, and, by the time he returned in early July, the Yankees were looking for an alternative. Organizational pitching coach Billy Connors told Steinbrenner, "I can't guarantee you that Hutton isn't going to get hurt again."

Still, barely anyone had ever heard of Weathers, who, with a 2-2 record and 4.54 ERA, couldn't have been any improvement over Hutton. Before leaving for Florida, Hutton told a reporter, "That's a trade I can't understand. I mean, what's the big deal about Weathers?"

After initially pitching terribly for the Yankees, Weathers would become an unsung hero in the postseason. But it was Fielder who'd have the greatest impact. The moment he walked through the clubhouse door in Texas, it was clear the Yankees had a leader—or, at the very least, someone who had presence. For all their talent, for all their collective professionalism, the Yankees were remarkably homogenous. Since Don Mattingly had left, no one had stepped forward to become the unquestioned leader.

Tino Martinez was still exorcising Mattingly's ghost at first base. Bernie Williams was too shy. Strawberry was struggling just to stay sober and drug-free. And Wade Boggs was simply too eccentric and had been embarrassed by a lawsuit that had just been filed by a Continental Airlines flight attendant who claimed Boggs had harassed and verbally abused her on a charter flight earlier in the season.

Even in his nickname, "Big Daddy," Fielder stood out. And the way he used the English language was, well, unique. A reporter who visited Fielder's locker for a pregame chat was greeted thus: "What's up, man? Wanna vibe?"

It took only a few minutes to realize there was a difference between a conversation with Fielder and one with Bernie Williams or John Wetteland. "To vibe" meant to talk. That was the first lesson. "Big Daddy" was a nickname he acquired at Class AA in 1984, when he was still the property of the Blue Jays. And Fielder proudly said, "You gotta be doing something good, something very cool, to get a name like 'Big Daddy' or 'Big Hurt.' That's what Frank Thomas is always telling me. It means things are cool."

Fielder looked around the room and noted, "Everyone is chillin' right now, then when it's game time, it's business. No one here gets overgeeked. And my man Cone ain't even here yet."

Throwing his head back and laughing loudly, Fielder said, "Coney's my dog," quickly explaining that being "overgeeked" meant being overexcited and that if someone was Fielder's "dog," then he was a friend. And that playing for the Yankees "was totally funked."

Is it any wonder the Yankees thought they'd clinched the division, acquiring a power hitter who was also the prime minister of cool? Even at Camden Yards, the Orioles were awed. "It sure looks like the Yankees are serious about this thing, getting Big Daddy," Bobby Bonilla told Baltimore reporters.

At the same time, however, the Yankees were getting their first hint that the road to October would not be smooth. After losing two of three to the Rangers, they would lose the first two games of a four-game set with the Royals. Although their lead was still relatively safe, it was impossible not to notice the metamorphosis.

These weren't the same Yankees who'd whipped through the first half of the season and certainly not the same team that had swept the Orioles a month earlier. Suddenly, the Yankees were nine ahead of Baltimore, the first time their lead had slipped under double figures since July 22.

"I never said the second half was going to be as easy as the first," said Joe Torre, who did his best to remain calm, lighting up another cigar, and reminding the beat guys that, barring a catastrophe, the Yankees were "still in the driver's seat."

Even so, there were some chilling glimpses into the future. In Texas, Mariano Rivera had been devoured by the Rangers' Juan Gonzalez, and, for the first time, the Yankees realized that the skinny little right-hander was human.

Who could have blamed the Yankees for believing otherwise? Listed at 168 pounds, but closer to 155, Rivera was a modern-day Ron Guidry—all arms and legs, not an ounce of muscle, but the owner of a fastball so fierce that opponents were batting just .191 against him.

Rivera, a native of Panama, had the rare gift of being able to throw a rising fastball. Although physicists have long insisted such a phenomenon is impossible, hitters swear that in the last five feet to the plate, Rivera's fastball rises from the belt to eye level.

There's no way to teach a pitcher to throw that way; it's a natural blessing that, over time, will evaporate. Dwight Gooden would watch Rivera and shake his head, recalling his own youth. "Mariano better appreciate what he's got, man, because it doesn't last," Doc said. "I remember when I could throw like that. But you wake up one day and you realize your ball doesn't move anymore, and then you're in deep shit unless you figure out a new pitch."

Rivera would listen to the advice and promise to work on a change-up or split-finger fastball—someday in the future. But now he had all the arrogance that a ninety-five-mph fastball instills in a young pitcher. Without embarrassment or self-consciousness, Rivera would smile and say, "When I've got my stuff, no one can hit my fastball. I can throw it by anyone I want."

But not on this night against Texas, and certainly not against Gonzalez. Rivera had inherited a 5–2 lead in the sixth inning from Kenny Rogers, and in the eighth inning, the Rangers went berserk. They got consecutive singles from Darryl Hamilton, Ivan Rodriguez, and Rusty Greer and then a devastating double off Gonzalez's bat that went hurtling into the center-field wall.

That narrowed the Yankees' lead to 6–4, and even though they held on for a 6–5 win, Rivera was officially beginning his first slump of 1996. Afterward he admitted that Gonzalez was too hot, even for him, and that the Rangers' right fielder "just beat me."

"I gotta give the guy credit. No one can get him out right now," Rivera said. "But I'm not worried because everything's cool. My arm feels fine. Fastball is fine. I'll get him next time."

But the next night, in Kansas City, Rivera was mauled again. For the first nine innings, Gooden and Kevin Appier staged a personal one-on-one war, matching each other inning for inning, and in the ninth, the game was still scoreless. Finally, in the tenth, Fielder led off with a massive home run to left off reliever Jeff Montgomery, and, when Derek Jeter added a two-run inside-the-park homer in the same inning, Rivera had a 3–0 lead and all he had to do was whip through the last three KC batters. Incredibly, the Royals were able to solve Rivera, just as the Rangers had. Four of the first five batters he faced reached base, and the final blow came on Keith Lockhart's single to left. With Jose Offerman on first, two out, and the score tied at 3–3, Gerald Williams should have thrown the ball to third base. Instead, he foolishly attempted to throw out Lockhart as he tried to stretch his single into a double. Williams, a former pitcher at Grambling who could reach ninety mph on the radar gun, was so in love with his throwing arm that he took it as an insult when a runner tried to advance on him.

So with the game on the line, Williams took the bait, firing a perfect strike to second base in his attempt to cut down Lockhart. Unfortunately for the Yankees, the throw was not only late but Offerman, taking advantage of Williams's poor decision, broke for the plate. Suddenly, the game turned into a race between Offerman's legs and second baseman Andy Fox's arm, and when Offerman slid under Joe Girardi's tag, the Royals nearly crushed him in a riot of high-fives.

The mighty Yankees had been beaten, and so had Rivera, the suddenly not-so-bulletproof reliever. Afterward Torre bluntly said Williams "made a mistake. He threw to the wrong base, and he knows it."

Williams took full responsibility. In fact, he sat in a corner of the clubhouse, his face buried in his hands, while teammates took turns consoling him. First Darryl Strawberry, then Dwight Gooden, then Derek Jeter, all telling Williams there would be many, many other chances for redemption.

But what of Rivera? He stonewalled any suggestion of a slump, insisting, "Everything is fine. They just got a couple of lucky hits off me. This game is my fault, not Gerald's, but there's nothing wrong with my arm."

A Rivera slump wasn't as easy for the Yankees to digest as a physical mistake by Williams. The ramifications were so dark that Torre simply said, "It's something that I don't want to think about. I'll just forget this one and come back strong tomorrow. What we'd like to get now is a strong game from Weathers. That will help a lot."

Indeed, with Rivera unavailable that night and John Wetteland suffering from the flu, this would be a perfect time for the former Marlin to shine. Weathers would be able to take pressure off the bull pen for a night and make Watson look smart for trading for him. The scouting report suggested Weathers might have luck against most American League hitters, who as a whole are in love with swinging for the fences.

Weathers was a sinker baller whose strength was in getting ground balls. Trouble was, the Royals were more like a National League team than any American League club. They hit the fewest home runs in the American League, happy just to make contact, put the ball in play, and force the defense into mistakes.

The night turned into a disaster for Weathers. Offerman, leading off in the first inning, hit his first pitch into center field, stole second, moved to third when Johnny Damon bounced to Tino Martinez, and scored when Bip Roberts—surely the league's frailest cleanup hitter—hit a sacrifice bloop into shallow center.

Jeter ended up catching the ball but had no chance to nail the speedy Offerman, who was tagging. That was pure National League baseball, and it was cutting Weathers to pieces. In the second inning, Weathers collapsed entirely as he hit Michael Tucker to start another outburst. Two outs later, the Royals strung together three straight singles and Torre was on his way out of the dugout, down 3–0, to take the ball out of Weathers's hands.

It was an embarrassing moment, both for the Yankees and their new right-hander. The rest of the bull pen was flogged, too, and when the Yankees lost, 11–4, they were in trouble for the first time all summer. Maybe not in the standings since they were still nine games up, but spiritually something was missing.

"We're a little flat right now," Torre conceded.

"Flat? We stink," Gooden said. "Good thing we have a big lead over Baltimore right now because we can't beat anyone. Not even these guys."

One more time, as they had all summer, the Yankees turned their lonely eyes to Andy Pettitte and, without ever having to say it, sent a message: Help.

The secret to throwing the cut-fastball is to just throw it. Don't snap the wrist, don't treat it like a slider or a curveball. Simply hold the ball off-center, put pressure on the index finger, and throw the ball as if it were a fastball.

If a pitcher stays true to those instructions, not only can the cutter be a devastating pitch but it puts virtually no strain on the elbow or shoulder. Of course, the temptation is always great to squeeze a little extra from the pitch—to make it break just an extra inch or two, to make it that much more unhittable. And when that happens, the wrist snaps down and the pitch actually becomes an elbow-taxing slider.

A pitcher isn't aware that he's traumatizing his arm; he only notices that the ball has a delicious, additional bite. So he keeps throwing it. But over the years, the body pays the surcharge. The most obvious example is Jim Abbott, the former Yankee who used to throw in the low nineties.

Not only could Abbott throw hard, but he had a cut-fastball that devoured right-handed hitters. The ball would start to cut midway to the plate, and, at the last moment, it would move three to four inches, just enough to jam a hitter and force a ground ball to third. But the more successful he became, the more Abbott demanded of the cutter, throwing it harder and harder until one day he lost his fastball. "Damn shame, but we saw it coming," said one Yankee coach. "Jim fell in love with the damned pitch until it ruined him."

Barely throwing eighty-one mph in 1996, Abbott had become the major league's losingest pitcher, an astonishing 1-15 when the Angels finally sent him to the minor leagues. Somewhere there was a lesson in all this for Andy Pettitte, who, like

Abbott, once upon a time was a talented lefty who had the gift of the cut-fastball.

Pettitte was cool and anxiety-free and felt he could rule the inside corner on righties—if not the world. He threw cutter after cutter, and as he took the mound against the Royals on August 4, he wasn't about to change his game plan. But that's not to say the alarm hadn't already been sounded.

For the month of July, Pettitte suffered his first sore arm. He didn't know where it came from, or what to do about it, only that, in his words, "It was driving me crazy. I thought my career was over." The Yankees took one MRI, then another, and were relieved to learn there was nothing wrong with Pettitte's elbow that a little rest wouldn't cure. That, and a few less cutters.

But that wasn't about to happen—certainly not when the Yankees were leaning so heavily on Pettitte for a win. By the time the season was over, thirteen of Pettitte's twenty-one wins would come after a Yankee loss, and there's no question that when Pettitte struck out two Royals in the first inning, the Yankees were saying a silent prayer of thanks.

In fact, the Yankees went on to an easy 5–3 win over the Royals, a machinelike affair that reminded everyone of the first half of the season. Mariano Duncan smoked an RBI double in a four-run fourth, and Derek Jeter's RBI single made it 5–0.

The rest of the afternoon was a living advertisement as to why Pettitte would end up as the American League's winningest pitcher. He struck out eleven Royals, and KC manager Bob Boone said, "He's got the most incredible breaking stuff I've seen this year. It's there one second, gone the next. I keep telling my guys, 'Lay off that thing.' But it's sure a lot easier said than done."

Pettitte threw seven blemish-free innings, striking out two more in the seventh. Pettitte broke a cutter over the inside corner on Joe Randa, the final batter, and the best the Royals' third baseman could do was a weak fly ball to right. There was nothing spectacular about that at-bat, except that, as he walked off the mound, Pettitte shook his left arm as if something was wrong.

Later, he insisted, "It was nothing. Nothing at all." Probably not. Maybe just a momentary visit from Jim Abbott's ghost.

George Steinbrenner

9

The Crisis

All summer the Yankees had been dreading that second West Coast trip. Their only hope? By the time they stepped inside their personal torture chamber, the Kingdome, the lead over the Orioles would be fat enough to withstand a disaster. And the Yankees felt one was coming.

Already the month of August was turning ugly on Joe Torre. Between August 4 and August 20, the Yankees' lead had been trimmed from ten games to six, thanks to a devastating four-game series against Seattle at the stadium. The Mariners took the first three games, scoring twenty-five runs, prompting Darryl Strawberry to admit, "They seem to have our number this year. I just can't explain it."

The Mariners were equal-opportunity Yankee thrashers: they nailed Kenny Rogers for eight runs in three innings on August 17, then pounded Dwight Gooden for seven runs and ten hits in just two and two-thirds innings the next night. No one had an antidote for Alex Rodriguez's bat speed, or Edgar Martinez's remarkable plate coverage, or Ken Griffey's overall star quotient. The Mariners were big and tough, the West's version of the Orioles. Not even Gooden's fastball could stop Seattle. In fact, Gooden's loss on the eighteenth dropped his record to 10-5, and while that was still more than respectable, George Steinbrenner was beginning to lose patience with his national celebrity.

Ever since the May 14 no-hitter, Gooden had become a spokesman for second chances. He said yes to virtually every interview request—TV, radio, newspapers, magazines, everyone wanted to chronicle this storybook resurrection. By the time the summer was over, Gooden was on the cover of *The Sporting News* and *New York* magazine, and he would soon be featured on ABC's documentary prime-time show *Turning Point*.

The producers wanted to spend a full hour on the dual sagas of Gooden and Strawberry, starting from their childhoods, and then follow with their high school careers, their early days with the Mets, their fall to cocaine, and their subsequent resurrections. Gooden, of course, was more than happy to participate, but he was stunned to discover that Steinbrenner not only was opposed to it but actually forbade him from speaking to ABC.

What was really bothering Steinbrenner was Gooden's involvement in an even larger project. Less than a week after Gooden's no-hitter, Doc had been contacted by movie producer Norman Twain, who had the idea of turning his life story into a feature-length film. Twain, who had produced the highly successful film *Lean on Me*, said Gooden's story "was perfect for Hollywood. It's really a very distinct three-act screenplay: the rise, the fall, and the return to baseball ending with the no-hitter."

And he was right. Not long after Twain's first call, Gooden sold the rights to his story to Warner Bros., and there was talk of Denzel Washington taking the leading role. Doc was so intrigued by the cinematic possibilities that he would eventually have lunch with Washington and take a walking tour of the Warner studios. But Steinbrenner was irritated by the outside interests that kept tugging on Gooden.

So irritated that following the August 18 13–12 loss to the Mariners, in which Gooden was ambushed for four runs in the first inning and Ken Griffey's two-run homer in the second, Steinbrenner picked up the telephone in his office in the stadium, called down to the clubhouse, and made equipment man Nick Priore find Gooden's friend and adviser Ray Negron.

Negron wasn't far away. In fact, he was at Gooden's locker at that very moment, helping the Doctor sort out the pounding he'd just absorbed from Seattle's hitters. Priore poked his head around the corner and said, "Ray, telephone for you."

The adviser took the phone. "Negron here."

"That was a fucking disgrace out there!" a voice screamed from the other end of the line. "If I have to hear one more thing about that fucking movie, you're both gone!"

As was his custom, Steinbrenner never identified himself, but Negron knew exactly who it was. And Negron further knew he was no match for Steinbrenner's rage, so he allowed him to hang up without saying a word and returned to Gooden's locker.

"What was that about?" Doc asked.

"Ah, nothing," Negron answered casually. "George just wanted to know how your arm felt."

Negron weighed whether to tell Doc the truth but asked himself what the point was. How would it benefit the emotionally fragile Gooden to know that Steinbrenner had turned his infamous temper on him? Would that make him pitch any better? Would it make the tendinitis in his shoulder disappear?

Truth was, Gooden's real enemy was the number of innings in his shoulder, not any TV interview or movie project. He'd been throwing for nearly an entire year without rest and was desperate for time off. But it was impossible for Gooden to make that request, not now, not with David Cone still on the disabled list and the Yankee lead shrinking by the day.

Gooden wanted to tell Steinbrenner that his involvement with Hollywood was, if anything, therapeutic. "Talking about my problems kept me focused on what I had to do to stay sober," he said. "It was a reminder about how far I'd let myself go and to never go back there again."

Actually, Steinbrenner had a larger issue to resolve, and that was the Mariners themselves. The scars from the '95 play-offs were still so fresh that, even a year later, the Yankees seemed intimidated. Jeff Nelson would know, having seen the Yankees' fear as a Mariner the year before, witnessing the Yankee meltdown in games three, four, and five of the play-offs.

Even after the Yankees had won the first two games of that series, Nelson said, "We knew we had them beat once we got them in our building. There was no way the Yankees were going to [beat] us. I mean, we hadn't won a game yet in the series, and, in our minds, the thing was over.

"The Mariners never feared anyone, or any team, but all we ever heard was the Yankees didn't want to come into the Dome and they didn't want to face Randy [Johnson]. It played right into our hands. Looking back, it shouldn't have been that big of a deal."

But it was, even in 1996. Johnson lost most of the summer to a bad back but was still trying to work himself into the rotation in mid-August. In fact, "The Big Unit" appeared in that August 18 game in the sixth inning, with the Mariners ahead, 10–8. Although Johnson was less than perfect, allowing Cecil Fielder a two-run single that tied the game at 10–10, he still struck out Strawberry, Joe Girardi, and Derek Jeter in the seventh inning.

Johnson would finally succumb to back surgery in September and miss the rest of the season, but his mere appearance was enough to remind the Yankees they were still carrying excess emotional baggage. And the burden became heavier three days later when the Yankees were crushed, 7–1, by the Angels and a rookie pitcher named Jason Dickson, cutting their lead to just five games.

Although Torre kept telling the press this was a slump, not a crisis, there was panic in the front office. On August 24, the Yankees acquired left-hander Graeme Lloyd and utility man Pat Listach from the Brewers in exchange for Bob Wickman and Gerald Williams. Bob Watson had decided he couldn't stomach much more of Wickman's on-again, off-again sinker, although he was the most durable of the Yankee relievers. And Williams, who batted .317 in the first half, was in a 5-for-50 slump and lost virtually all his playing time to Strawberry.

Only what were the Yankees getting in return? Lloyd, a 6' 7" collection of arms and legs and the owner of an adequate sinking fastball, had pitched reasonably well for Milwaukee. But that was in the low-pressure setting of County Stadium. Listach was also regarded as a useful infielder/outfielder, but, as the Yankees were soon to find out, nothing about this trade would turn out right.

The turbulence became so severe that two days later Wally Whitehurst was summoned from Class AAA Columbus to start against the A's. This was the same Whitehurst who was once a promising right-hander for the Mets in the eighties but ended up bouncing around the minor leagues in the Padres, Giants, and Expos systems. Finally, in the middle of the summer, Whitehurst hooked on with the Yankees affiliate and was just as surprised as anyone that he was summoned to the Bronx on such short notice.

When Whitehurst first walked through the clubhouse doors, he sought out his old pitching coach Mel Stottlemyre and teammates Darryl Strawberry and Dwight Gooden.

"Doc, who's ordering the pizza?" Whitehurst asked with a smile, referring to the Shea Stadium custom from another era, when the pitchers used to send a clubhouse kid out for several pies to be delivered to the bull pen.

Gooden's jaw dropped at Whitehurst's question.

"Wally, this ain't the Mets," Doc said. "We don't do shit like that here."

These were the Yankees, the world's most famous and prestigious sports franchise. Nevertheless, Whitehurst was still forced to wear the oversized pants of former pitcher Rich Monteleone. And when the cap assigned him didn't fit, he had to send a clubhouse kid upstairs to the stadium souvenir shop to find him one that did.

Astoundingly, Whitehurst went seven innings and allowed the A's just two runs as the Yankees went on to a 5–4 win. The right-hander would be returned to the minors after getting pounded five days later, but he had slowed the Yankee slide for one night. But a loss to Oakland the next day, which represented the end of the homestand, again cut their lead to five games. The Yankees quietly packed their bags, headed for their charter bus to Newark airport, boarded the 727 aircraft, and contemplated the 2,500-mile journey to the Pacific Northwest.

The sign appears in a player's line of sight the moment he walks into the Kingdome's visiting clubhouse: WELCOME BACK TO SEATTLE! Beneath those words are clubhouse man Scott Gilbert's name. Although the sign is left posted all year for every visiting team to see—so players will know whose name to write on the checks when it comes time to leave a tip—the Yankees wondered if there was a tweak.

After all, who felt welcome in the Kingdome? In the very first inning of the first game of the series on August 26, Jimmy Key was struck on the left elbow by Alex Rodriguez's line drive. It was an awful sight: the ball coming off Rodriguez's bat in a blur, hitting Key so hard that it ricocheted all the way to the wall in right-center.

Key was forced to leave the game, but, for seven magical innings, Brian Boehringer paralyzed the Mariners with a ninety-one-mph fastball. It was a stunning transformation for the right-hander, who in the first half of the season was 0-2 with a 10.29 ERA. Boehringer was promptly returned to Columbus, where he was tutored by organizational pitching coach Billy Connors, and there he said, "I started to figure out what I should be doing with hitters, learning to think ahead in every situation."

Boehringer proved himself several times in the game. With no score in the fourth inning, he struck out the dangerous Jay Buhner with Griffey on third and Edgar Martinez on second. Boehringer again threw a fastball by Buhner in the sixth inning, stranding Martinez on first base, and, after a scoreless seventh, left the game after getting Rodriguez to fly out to right in the eighth.

The Yankees had taken a 1–0 lead in the seventh inning, which meant that after Rodriguez's fly ball, they were just five outs away from breaking the Kingdome's hex. Torre came to the mound and summoned the newcomer from Milwaukee, Lloyd, to deal with Griffey.

Ordinarily the game would have been the property of Mariano Rivera by now. Rivera had come back from his brief slump to dominate again. But since John Wetteland had gone on the disabled list August 16 with a groin injury, Rivera had to be used as the closer. Wetteland's injury had a disastrous ripple effect, for without Rivera to rescue starters in the seventh or eighth inning, no lead was safe.

Here was a prime example, as Torre was forced to rely on Lloyd in such a critical spot. Strategically, the move made sense—at least because Lloyd was a lefty and so was Griffey. But it turned out to be a mismatch. Lloyd seemed so intimidated by Griffey that he walked him on five pitches, leaving Dave Pavlas to deal with Martinez. That, too, resulted in a walk, and when Buhner and Brian Hunter followed with back-to-back RBI singles, the Yankees were on their way to a shocking 2–1 loss.

The next night was just as disastrous, as Kenny Rogers collapsed after five scoreless innings. Rogers allowed Rich Amaral a leadoff home run, a double to Rodriguez, and, one out later, an RBI single to Martinez. Jeff Nelson surrendered a single to Buhner, and once again Lloyd was pummeled, allowing Jeff Manto a two-run homer.

After the game, Lloyd's voice was barely better than a whisper as he admitted that "something was wrong" in the way he was pitching, the way his arm felt, even in his equilibrium on the mound. "I don't feel very comfortable," he said. "I have to remind myself this is the same game of baseball that I've been playing all these years with the Brewers."

Not exactly. This was the Yankee universe, a fiefdom ruled by You Know Who. The next day, Jim Salisbury of the *Post* and Jack Curry of the *Times* reported that Steinbrenner had harsh words for Rogers for his inability to better his game during a collapse. Rogers seemed to be in a complete daze, insisting that there was nothing wrong with his arm and that he was simply beaten by good hitters using their skills on otherwise good pitches.

Rogers, as he would admit three weeks later in Toronto, was not being entirely truthful. He was suffering from inflammation in the left shoulder, the result of that line-drive injury he received in spring training. His mechanics were slightly askew after that, and, as Rogers would confess in a private moment, "My arm hasn't really felt right all year."

He wasn't the only one with shoulder problems. Gooden was also the victim of a tired arm. Yet he wasn't about to run to the trainers. "My whole life I've been taught to keep pitching, keep competing, never give up," Gooden said. "I can't let this team down now. Not when we're in trouble like this."

Doc hadn't done much to lower his profile during this dead-arm period. In fact, he had made national news two nights earlier when the Mets announced the firing of their manager, Dallas Green. For years, Doc had harbored a grudge against Green, and now he was ready to unload.

Gooden sidled up to John Giannone of the *Daily News* and Bob Klapisch of the Bergen *Record* and said, "You want to know what I think of that guy Green?" The two reporters could barely keep up with Doc's invective.

"A lot of times when people have their own problems, they start pointing fingers to get the attention away from themselves. Dallas's problems came from alcohol," Gooden said. "Some of the things he said about me . . . he needs to look in the mirror and check himself first.

"I have no respect for him, as a person or as a manager. The way he was with his players, he was your friend if you were going good. But if you went bad, he didn't want to talk to you anymore. It was 'we' if the team was winning, but as soon as it started losing, it was 'you.' It was never his fault. Nothing was ever his fault."

Gooden paused a moment, riffling through the files in his memory bank. He recalled an incident in the summer of '93, not long before he was suspended, in which he and Green nearly came to blows in the clubhouse. Doc had suffered what he called "a real bad game" against Florida and was "hung out to dry" by Green.

"I just didn't have it that day. It was just one of those things," Gooden said. "But he kept sending me out there every inning. I'll never forget that. After the game, he told the reporters, 'Gooden makes a lot of money, he should pitch a lot of innings.'

"I know I made a lot of money, but you don't do that to one of your own guys. I went up to him after that because I heard what he'd said to the press, and I told him, 'If you've got something to say, say it to my face.' "

Gooden ridiculed Green's "open-door" policy, saying, "It was open until he started ripping you. But he closed it if you tried to go in there and confront him." Doc once recalled an incident in which Jeromy Burnitz, then a promising young outfielder, challenged Green to a fight in the dugout, only to find the door to the manager's office closed after the game.

A day after his dismissal, Green was a guest on WFAN's Mike and the Mad Dog show, with hosts Mike Francesa and Chris Russo. Surprisingly, he let Gooden's comments pass without retaliation, although he had to enjoy Gooden's performance the next night, August 28, when Doc was outmuscled by the Mariners, who scored eight runs on nine hits—three of them home runs—in just five and two-thirds innings. That cut the Yankees' lead to just four games, and a combination of panic and frustration was everywhere in the organization.

It certainly manifested itself on the field that night in the eighth inning, when Paul O'Neill was buzzed by an up-and-in fastball thrown by Tim Davis. O'Neill, knocked to the ground, got up and stared directly into the Mariners' dugout, openly challenging Piniella, who he said "has been doing the same shit to me for three years. It's the same thing, year after year, and I'm tired of it."

O'Neill had played for Piniella from 1990 to 1992 in Cincinnati, and Sweet Lou had always told friends that, while talented, O'Neill had underachieved for years because of his sulking nature. Ever since both men had migrated to the American League, O'Neill was sure that Piniella had been trying to intimidate him with fastballs near his head.

To this, Piniella just laughed and said, "If I was going to throw at anyone, I sure wouldn't bring in my softest thrower to do it. And Tim Davis is my softest thrower." Nevertheless, words were exchanged between O'Neill and John Marzano, and within seconds O'Neill had wrestled the Seattle catcher to the ground. That started a massive brawl, which featured under-the-card bouts between Strawberry and reliever Bobby Ayala, O'Neill and left-hander Terry Mulholland, and O'Neill being separated from Piniella.

Although no one was seriously injured, the hostility between the two teams approached outright hatred.

Piniella told reporters that O'Neill was a "crybaby" and that if he didn't like being pitched inside, "then he should stop crying, get in the batter's box, and hit one off the wall."

Mariano Duncan, who played for Piniella in Cincinnati, called Sweet Lou "the biggest fucking jerk I've ever met in baseball."

Jimmy Leyritz said, "If Piniella had come out of the dugout early in the fight, I guarantee Paulie would've taken him down. One on one, Paulie would've killed him."

Strawberry, who was attacked by a half dozen Mariners, said, "A lot of those guys talk a lot of trash, especially Mulholland and Bobby Ayala. Bring 'em on. They're sissies. I'll fight 'em all."

And Piniella defiantly said, "I'm not afraid of anyone" on the Yankees roster and taunted the Bombers by saying, "I never thought they were twelve games better than anyone in that division."

Piniella paced his office after the fight, half naked and pulling on a cigarette. He said, "Paul should stop crying so much. He'd be a heck of a ballplayer if he stopped. He already is, but he'd be even better if he stopped crying. But everyone in the league knows he likes to dive in on pitches, and pitchers are going to throw him inside because they know it'll frustrate him. If he would just step in the box, hit one off the wall, I guarantee you it would stop."

And the Yankee tough talk? Piniella smiled so broadly his eyes turned into slits. "Ah, that's just a lot of frustration. We've beaten them, what, seven of nine? They're just mad. They've lost a lot of games off their lead. Now they're in a race, and they don't like it."

As always, it took Joe Torre to put matters in perspective. Looking especially drawn and pale as the Yankees moved on to Anaheim, Torre said, "We're not playing well right now. A lot of things are going wrong, and it's frustrating. The Mariners kicked our butts in this series, and it leaves a bad taste in our mouths."

On August 30, Yankee PR director Rick Cerrone gathered the beat reporters in the middle of the visitors' clubhouse in Anaheim, cleared his throat, and produced a single sheet of paper.

"Guys, we have an announcement," Cerrone said.

At that moment Paul O'Neill walked by the flock of notebooks and asked loudly, "Who we trading for today?"

Cerrone looked up but didn't answer O'Neill. Instead, he cleared his throat one more time and delivered stunning news. Charlie Hayes had been acquired from the Pirates and, according to Torre, would begin sharing time with Wade Boggs at third base.

The Yankees themselves were stunned—not out of any great loyalty to Boggs but because of the apparent panic that had taken hold of the front office. Since July 29, the club had made thirteen personnel changes, hardly in keeping with Torre's credo that clubhouse patience and calm wins pennants, not the revolving-door policy that was now in effect.

But Torre insisted this addition was for Boggs's benefit, saying he thought the sure-thing Hall of Fame candidate had looked "a little tired lately." To this Boggs shot back, "Well, I'll get my three thousand hits somewhere," implying that his career with the Yankees had been forced to an end.

Then, to emphasize his displeasure with Torre, Boggs loudly summoned a clubhouse attendant to his locker, pointed to a stack of bats on the floor, and said, "I'm sorry, but do you think you could help me take those bats to the field? I'm too tired to carry them myself." Soon after, Boggs suffered a massive back spasm, which he intimated could have been caused by stress.

And Graeme Lloyd continued to stagger his way through the month of August. On the twenty-ninth, he failed to retire any of the four batters he faced and was charged with four runs in the Yankees' embarrassing 14–3 loss to the Angels.

After the game, Lloyd finally admitted the problem wasn't nerves or bad mechanics or bad karma. It was simply a bad arm: nine days before the Milwaukee trade, he'd received a cortisone shot in his elbow, a fact the Brewers conveniently forgot to mention to the Yankees. Already, Listach had arrived from the Brewers with a broken foot, a fracture that wasn't detected by either the Yankees or the Brewers until a second and third set of X rays. General Manager Sal Bando sent over right-hander Ricky Bones as compensation.

But Lloyd's injury enraged Bob Watson, who could only take Bando's word that he'd been dealing with healthy players. Unlike the NBA or the NFL, which stipulates that no trade can be completed until the players involved pass a physical, baseball executives operate on good faith, and, as Watson put it, "If the man [Bando] tells me I'm getting a healthy player, there's not much I can do about it except take his word."

But that explanation hardly satisfied Steinbrenner, who felt the Yankees had been publicly embarrassed by a smaller, second-tier organization. One Yankee source, in fact, said Watson was "already gone" and could only save his job by winning the World Series.

Strangely, Watson did nothing to lower the temperature around this controversy. "If we blow a twelve-game lead, Joe and I deserve to get fired," he said. "You don't blame the passengers when a plane crashes. We fly the plane."

The messier the Yankee landscape became, the more obvious it became a savior was needed.

David Cone was in a cab by 7 A.M. outside his Manhattan apartment, on his way to LaGuardia, ready to begin a cross-country, one-man rescue mission. His recovery from shoulder surgery had been fast and, as far as the doctors knew, perfect. In two minor-league starts at Class AA Norwich, Cone had allowed just one earned run in ten innings, but that was no barometer. What he really wanted was a chance to resuscitate the Yankees.

Initially, the Yankees had wanted Cone to wait until September 6. But here it was, September 1, and the call for help had been made. "What was the use of waiting?" he asked. "It was obvious my arm was fine, so why waste the innings in the minor leagues?"

A day later Cone proved that miracles sometimes do occur. He stepped onto the mound at the Oakland Coliseum and rewound the clock to 1988. Everything he threw was a strike, every pitch moved at the last second, and even his fastball had a little extra octane. In seven innings the A's still didn't have a hit.

It was a special afternoon. So magical that Cone and Torre smiled uncomfortably at each other in the dugout in the eighth inning, neither man able to find the right words for what was going to be an awkward moment. How does a manager tell his pitcher to forget a no-hitter after seven innings? How does a pitcher beg for a part of history?

"That's gonna be it, David," Torre said. "You're at eighty-five [pitches] already. We can't push it."

"You know, it's possible I could have a quick eighth," Cone said hopefully.

"Even if you do, you still won't pitch the ninth," the manager said softly.

Cone, exhaling slowly, slumping in defeat, finally said, "It's your call. If you leave it up to me, I'm going out there. So it's your call."

That's how Cone's comeback ended, a 5–0 win over the A's that became the year's greatest what-if question. Cone could only watch from the dugout as the Yankees' bid for a combined no-hitter, which would have been the tenth in franchise history, ended with Jose Herrera's infield single off Mariano Rivera in the ninth inning.

With Cone out, the no-hitter didn't matter so much. The Yankees had other matters in their consciousness now. As Rivera put it, "The reason David came back was to help us win. That's what matters. The worst is over."

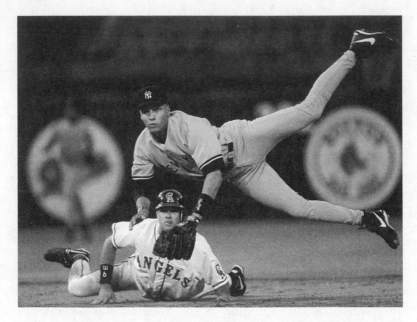

Derek Jeter

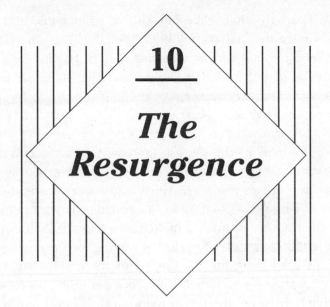

10

The Resurgence

T he visitors' clubhouse in dilapidated Tiger Stadium is about the size of a two-car garage. Put a temporary row of lockers in the middle of the room to accommodate September call-ups, add forty players, coaches, and trainers, and the place feels like a crowded F train. Let in a frenzied New York media contingent and you've got one of those old college fraternity gags: how many people can we squeeze into a phone booth?

For a ball club teetering on the verge of a historic collapse, the atmosphere was nothing short of claustrophobic. Nerves were frayed and emotions were running high as the Yankees arrived in Detroit on September 10, their lead down to two and a half games over the Orioles.

If ever players needed their space, now was the time, but there was none to be found in this old dungeon of a dressing room. By four-thirty in the afternoon, players couldn't make a move without bumping into one another or, worse, a reporter.

This is what irritates the hell out of ballplayers, and you could almost hear what they were thinking: *The game is three hours from starting; why in the name of Billy Martin—he'd kick some ass in here right now if he were still alive—do these lowlife media people need to be standing around the clubhouse, most of them doing nothing more than telling jokes to one another and listening in on our conversations?* The problem is that stand-around time is one of the evils of the job for sportswriters, especially New York writers, who need material for early-edition stories that are written before the seven-thirty game even starts. Sometimes it's a matter of waiting for a particular player to emerge from the trainer's room and make himself available for an interview. Other times it's a matter of waiting for the manager to hold his daily pregame briefing. And then there are times when it's purely a matter of New York paranoia, no reporter wanting to leave while the competition is still in the room on the smallest chance that, say, a brawl could break out between Darryl Strawberry and Dwight Gooden.

Most modern clubhouses are big enough so reporters can stand around mostly unnoticed. But not this one, especially since six of the eight papers that cover the Yankees on the road had sent a columnist in addition to their beat reporter, as the pennant race continued to become a hotter story by the day.

In the middle of this vortex, Joe Torre, as usual, was a picture of tranquillity. Already he had shown remarkable poise and patience through the kind of slide that would have turned many a manager into either a recluse hiding in his office or a raging maniac battling daily with the press. Torre never let anyone see him sweat, not even his players.

On this day he made a point of being as visible as possible. He made the rounds in the clubhouse, kidding Andy Pettitte about a new haircut, asking Darryl Strawberry how his aching Achilles tendons were holding up. He chatted individually with a handful of different reporters at various checkpoints around the clubhouse, even though he would also hold a formal group press session in the dugout in an hour.

From a corner of the clubhouse, pitching coach Mel Stottlemyre watched Torre with much admiration.

"He hasn't changed a bit through this whole thing," Stottlemyre said quietly. "Players pick up on that. They know when you're panicking, when you start doing things differently. They smell it right away. It hasn't happened with Joe, and I think this team will respond to him."

By four forty-five Torre's presence was about all that was keeping the more hostile of the Yankee players from declaring war on all the notebooks and tape recorders. As it was, a few were grumbling about "getting the buzzards out of here." Torre sensed the growing tension and ambled over to PR director Rick Cerrone.

"Let's get everybody out of here in ten minutes," Torre said quietly. "We're gonna have a meeting."

Torre had been planning a meeting anyway. He thought it was time. An off day had given him plenty of time to consider what he wanted to say to his players after they had stumbled again, losing two of three at home to the Toronto Blue Jays. He understood the anxiety his players were feeling and knew instinctively that any sort of stern lecture would be counterproductive. He also knew that too much of a rah-rah speech would sound false at this point, out of character for him.

Still, Torre's managing style all season had been based on the trust he had in his players, and he sensed that they needed to hear him say he still believed in them. So when they gathered around, Torre told them flatly: "We're gonna win this thing."

Five times he repeated the line, during his fifteen minutes of talking, while urging the Yankees to play with the arrogance of a first-place team that fully expected to win. Take the extra base, he told his players. Play boldly.

"Turn it loose," he concluded. "We've got three weeks left. Now's the time. We're gonna win this thing."

The Yankees seemed to get the message. They came out swinging at the first good pitch they saw from Todd Van Poppel that night, hitting ropes all over the ballpark while scoring three runs in the top of the first.

Only one problem: no amount of inspiration could help Dwight Gooden. He took the mound with a 3–0 lead, and, for the first time in his major-league career, he couldn't get out of the first inning. The radar gun clocked his fastball at ninety-two mph, but that's why baseball people rarely rely strictly on the gun in judging a pitcher. Whatever the speed, Gooden's fastball was straight and flat.

"The pop ain't there" was the way Doc would describe it afterward. "The ball just wasn't coming out of my hand."

Torre didn't need a gun to see it from the dugout. Four batters into the game, when Tony Clark drilled a two-run double into the right-field corner, Torre got Ricky Bones up in the bull pen.

"I'd never do that so early with a pitcher like Dwight Gooden unless I was concerned about what I was seeing," Torre would say afterward. "There was just nothing there."

Three batters later, a right-handed hitter named Phil Hiatt rocked a Gooden fastball as if it had been placed on a tee for him, drilling it 420 feet to dead center for a triple. And out came Torre. After the game Gooden was asked if he was offended at receiving such a quick hook. Doc smiled a sad smile and said, "I'm surprised he didn't come get me earlier."

The lead was gone along with Gooden, and you could see shoulders sag around the infield. At least a couple of players would admit privately to wondering, as they watched Gooden disappear into the dugout, if they were powerless to stop this collapse. The good vibes from Torre's meeting had given way to a sense of helplessness.

"If you had to pick a time when our season was really on the line," Strawberry would say in October, "that might have been it. Seeing Doc get knocked out like that was hard. Things weren't going well as it was. It was a big test for us. We knew we couldn't lose to Detroit, or everything might have snowballed."

They hadn't been hitting much; indeed, they'd been handcuffed in New York by a couple of journeymen, Paul Quantrill and Erik Hanson. But they knew they'd have to rescue their season on this night with their bats, and they did. They pounded Van Poppel to take an 8–6 lead after five innings, and from there Brian Boehringer and Jeff Nelson carried the game to their late-inning warriors, Mariano Rivera and John Wetteland, who was just back after three weeks on the disabled list.

Only it wasn't over. With the score 9–8, Wetteland got in trouble in the ninth, walking two straight Tiger hitters with one out. Bobby Higginson then lined a bullet to right that looked like a sure game-tying single.

But out of nowhere came Ruben Rivera. After all these months, a new savior emerged. Again destiny seemed to be at work. Had Pat Listach not arrived from Milwaukee with a broken bone in his foot, Rivera might well have been sent home to Panama rather than called up to New York after the Triple A season ended in Columbus.

Bob Watson said as much the day of the fateful deal with the Brewers. Rivera was the Yankees' top prospect, a true five-tool blue-chipper, but he had been disciplined by Columbus manager Stump Merrill a couple of times, essentially for what was considered a bad attitude. And he had hit only .235 with ten home runs, a terribly disappointing season.

Watson was in agreement with the Yankee minor-league directors that Rivera should not be rewarded with a call-up. Steinbrenner would later say he would have insisted on it, claiming the kid was misunderstood, but that was after Rivera had helped win two big September games. The Boss may not have been so magnanimous at the time a decision had to be made.

But with Gerald Williams gone to Milwaukee and Listach injured, the Yankees desperately needed help in the outfield. So here was Rivera, newly inserted for Paul O'Neill, who was nursing a hamstring injury. Blessed with great instincts and first-step quickness, Rivera reacted instantly to the liner, sprinted four steps to his right, and made a diving catch to avoid disaster. Wetteland then got Mark Lewis to ground out to Derek Jeter, and the Yankees rushed to mob Rivera.

The sense of relief in the clubhouse was overwhelming. The Orioles had won again, but the Yankees needed a win to restore some self-esteem, even if the opponent was the worst team in baseball.

"It wasn't pretty, but we showed some guts," said Mariano Duncan. "That's what counts. It feels good."

But out in the hallway, Dwight Gooden felt nothing but emptiness. He talked like a man who knew his season was over. He hadn't felt strong for a couple of weeks, and even with an extra two days of rest this time, he felt as though he were throwing a grapefruit. "It doesn't hurt," he said. "There's just nothing there. It's frustrating. To come all this way and not to be able to help in the big games, it's tough."

No one could say for sure why Gooden was on empty. An MRI would show inflammation in his shoulder, but nothing alarming. It may have been simply that Gooden had been throwing hard for so long, first in an effort to convince teams to sign him after his suspension and then to impress the Yankees, that his arm needed a rest.

A between-starts throwing session two days later convinced Torre and Stottlemyre that Gooden should come out of the rotation. After ten days of rest Doc would get two more starts, and while he managed to get through five innings each time, it was obvious he wasn't right. Torre would have no choice but to take him off the postseason roster.

After all the hurdles, Gooden felt a powerful sense of letdown, yet he was warmed, too, by a sense of accomplishment.

Most important, he was clear, still committed to his one-day-at-a-time philosophy. And he'd made it back to the top, actually carrying the pitching staff for a period of about six weeks in May and June when every other starter was having one problem or another.

"I was as proud of that as I was of the no-hitter," Gooden would later say.

Eleven years had passed since his phenomenal Cy Young Award season. It had been ten years since the joyride with the '86 Mets and nine since he first tested positive for cocaine. After all this time, after nearly destroying his career and his life, Gooden had made a major contribution to a championship team. The thought would stay with him in October, dulling the ache of watching from the sidelines. That and the fact that George Steinbrenner told him he was picking up the option on his contract for 1997.

"I came a long, long way back," Gooden would say at the season's end. "Not all the way, but I'm not done yet either."

The Yankees came away from that first game in Detroit buoyed by the true grit they'd shown in overcoming Gooden's early knockout, but they weren't instantly transformed. They mud-wrestled with the Tigers through another ugly game the next night as well, and to win, 7–3, they needed their old "friend" Ruben Sierra to somehow fail to get a glove on a routine fly ball in the seventh inning that allowed two tie-breaking runs to score.

But that's the beauty of winning. It's a cure for the psyche, no matter the hows and whys. Suddenly, the clubhouse didn't seem too small. Suddenly, the room was filled with laughter again. Two wins was two wins, and when David Cone finessed his way to a third straight victory the next afternoon, a 12–3 laugher that featured eight RBIs from Bernie Williams, the Yankees again reeked of confidence.

"It was almost a must-sweep," Cone said that day. "And the way we did it, coming back to erase a couple of deficits, makes the whole team feel good about itself."

It was their first three-game winning streak in over a month, the first sign in weeks that a turnaround was coming. It was a time to exhale, so naturally everyone in the Yankee front office was hyperventilating.

Steinbrenner was still furious at Watson over the deal with the Brewers, screaming at him on a regular basis, according to many a Yankee employee. Then that week the Bergen *Record* reported that Steinbrenner had already decided he would fire Watson at the season's end. The *Record* cited anonymous sources in the Yankee organization as the source for the story.

Watson assumed the source was Steinbrenner, and he responded the next day with some ill-chosen comment in a story written by Jack Curry of *The New York Times*. First, Watson dragged Torre into his doghouse, implying that *both of them* should be fired if the Yankees failed to hold on down the stretch.

In addition, Watson challenged Steinbrenner, saying that rather than leak a story to the newspapers, "I would think he'd be enough of a man to come and tell me."

It seemed Watson had a professional death wish. Maybe he wanted to get fired—he had a second year guaranteed on his contract. Clearly he was tired of being Steinbrenner's punching bag. Watson was a proud man who'd had a nice career himself as a player before rising through the Houston Astros' organization to become the only black general manager in baseball. He understood when he was hired by the Yankees that there would be a price to pay for the prestige the title brought, but he had been on the job only a month when he found out just how high a price.

It was the day before Thanksgiving. Randy Velarde, a valuable Yankee utility player, signed with the California Angels largely because the Angels told him they wanted him to be their everyday second baseman. Steinbrenner was already reeling from criticism over cutting ties with Buck Showalter and Mike Stanley, and in recent days he'd told Watson to make sure he re-signed Velarde.

Watson had been reluctant to make Velarde any promises about playing time, but he didn't expect him to make such a quick decision. When the news broke, Watson was on his way home to Houston for the holiday. Hours later, upon learning of the Velarde signing himself, Steinbrenner ordered Watson to return to Yankee headquarters in Tampa and work out of the office over the Thanksgiving weekend.

Months later an acquaintance of Watson's said, "Bob knew right then he'd made a mistake. He wanted to quit right there."

Watson stayed on, however, and put up with Steinbrenner's badgering and second-guessing. So at this point his frustration was understandable, but by unfairly lumping Torre in with himself, Watson set off media alarms, and the manager found himself cornered by reporters before the final game of the Tigers series. Again, many managers would have been rattled by or just plain furious at the timing of the latest controversy. Torre remained as unflappable as ever, discussing the subject as casually as if he were talking about the weather, even offering Watson support.

"He goes through a lot more than I do," Torre said that day. "What is it they say, the mayor of New York has the second-toughest job in the country? Well, [Watson's job] ought to go right alongside that one. Hopefully, when this is all over, we can laugh about it."

A few hours later, with his first three-game winning streak in a month under his belt, Torre was smiling anyway. And when the Yankees went on to win three out of four games in Toronto, extending their winning streak to five games in the process, their second-half funk appeared to be history.

But the true test was at hand.

The Orioles came to town on September 17 convinced it would be different this time. In the two months since the Yankees had left them for dead, the Birds had swept their internal problems under a pile of home runs. This would be their best and last chance. They were the newly crowned kings of the long ball, having just broken the single-season record of 240 home runs set in 1961 by the Yankees of Mickey Mantle and Roger Maris fame. The O's would finish the season with 251 home runs, making them the most powerful team in baseball history.

Home runs had flown out of ballparks all around the majors in record numbers, but there was no disputing the Orioles' muscle, especially since their lineup of all-stars had been supplemented by in-season trades for Eddie Murray, Todd Zeile, and Pete Incaviglia. The power, plus the return from injury of hard-throwing relievers Alan Mills and Armando Benitez, fueled a six-week surge during which they went 31-15.

Ripples of turmoil still were felt around the ball club, however. Davey Johnson had gone ahead after the Yankee sweep in July and moved Cal Ripken to third base, but an intimidated Manny Alexander flopped so badly at short that the manager ended the experiment after eight games. Of course, it couldn't have helped that Ripken didn't so much as say hello to Alexander during that time.

Similarly, Johnson had ignored Mike Mussina's protests and implemented a four-man rotation, an idea that proved far more successful, coinciding with the Orioles' climb.

There had been other incidents as well. Scott Erickson had criticized the Orioles' defense as the reason his record wasn't better. More recently, after a tough loss that had dropped the O's to three and a half games behind the Yanks, Brady Anderson had gone to the official scorer on behalf of Ripken to argue that a play ruled an error should have been a hit for his buddy. And, Davey Johnson would bemoan privately, nobody was willing to hit the ball to the right side and give up a chance for a home run to move a runner over.

No wonder the Baltimore media had taken to calling them the "Tin Men"—a team with no heart.

Johnson himself insisted that a "mutual respect" had been forged over the summer between himself and his players, but the truth was the O's had merely overcome turmoil with talent. The Ripken faction of the clubhouse was still conducting a cold war with the manager, and Davey wasn't in love with some of his players, either. He had especially hard feelings toward Bobby Bonilla that went back to the early-season arguments over the designated-hitter role. While Johnson said publicly that he'd made a mistake forcing the designated-hitter role on Bonilla, he was telling friends he wanted no part of managing him for another season.

In fact, both he and General Manager Pat Gillick had agreed months earlier that the team would be better off without Bonilla and went about trying to trade him. Gillick told owner Peter Angelos in June he wanted to trade Bonilla for Eddie Murray, but Angelos vetoed the deal. Gillick went back to Angelos in late July, when it seemed the O's were out of contention, and said he wanted to trade Bonilla to the Reds for a couple of blue-chip prospects. Again Angelos, who had overruled his baseball people a year earlier in trading Alex Ochoa to the Mets for Bonilla, said no.

Now Angelos looked like a genius for insisting that Gillick drop deals that were in place for Bonilla and also left-hander David Wells. Both players had responded with strong second halves to help lead the Orioles' charge. For weeks the O's had pointed to this series in New York, hoping to be close enough to the Yankees to make them sweat. And indeed, at three games back, a sweep of the series would put them in a first-place tie.

But for all that had changed between the two teams, some vital elements remained the same. For one thing, the weather was lousy again, an all-day rain turning the first game of the series into a fiasco that never should have been started and was postponed after less than a full inning—just long enough to waste efforts from the respective aces, Mussina and Cone.

For another, the Yankees still owned the late innings, which is why Joe Torre continued to put so much trust in his ball club. So when the rain finally stopped the next night, September 18, the Yankees found themselves trailing 2–1 after eight innings, and yet Torre brought in Mariano Rivera to relieve Andy Pettitte in the top of the ninth. It was a gamble to use

Rivera in what looked like a losing cause because of the chance the outing might leave him unavailable for the rescheduled doubleheader the following day.

But Torre wanted to give his team every chance to win this one, and it paid off. Rivera got out of the ninth, and the Yankees rallied to tie in the bottom half, Bernie Williams muscling an inside fastball from Alan Mills up the middle for a game-tying single.

Rivera stayed in to pitch the tenth, and the Yanks won it in the bottom half. Again, Ruben Rivera, the kid up from Columbus, did the honors, punching a single to right against Mills to score Derek Jeter.

The win put the Yankees four games ahead and again brought out the worst in the Orioles. Randy Myers, the ex-Met who was one of the few Davey Johnson disciples in the ball club, lashed out at the manager after the game for pulling him in the ninth after he had walked Paul O'Neill and Cecil Fielder.

"The closer's job is to get three outs in the ninth inning without giving up the lead," Myers said that night, "and I wasn't given the chance to finish the job."

The writers covering the Orioles just rolled their eyes. Typical Birdland response in 1996. And they considered Myers one of the good guys in that clubhouse.

The Yankees allowed themselves a private snicker or two when Myers's comments made headlines the next day. Hunger outweighed ego on their side, and the Good Ship Torre continued to sail in smooth waters as a result.

The Bombers finished any hopes the Orioles had of winning the division by knocking out Mussina early in the first game of the doubleheader and routing them, 9–3. Then Cone, pitching on only a day's rest like Mussina, failed to hold a 6–1 lead in the nightcap and the Yankees blew the chance for another sweep, losing, 10–9.

But the deed had been done. The O's left town four games back, losers of ten of thirteen games with the Yankees, and once again the Yanks figured they'd seen the last of them. In their view, even if the Birds won the wild card, they weren't beating the Cleveland Indians.

More significantly, the American League East belonged to the boys from the Bronx. There was still the matter of clinching, but to a man the Yankees knew it was over.

They split four games at home with the Red Sox as the media counted down the magic number, and, fittingly, they clinched the division by winning the first game of a double-header against the Milwaukee Brewers on September 25 at the stadium, the result of still another rain-out a night earlier. The clincher was a whopping 19–2 win in what turned out to be one long night of celebration.

In the end, after Cone had pitched six innings to earn the victory, Torre had his choice of pitchers to pick from for the honor of being on the mound for the final out. He decided on right-hander Jeff Nelson, who had endured a fairly miserable season, failing to live up to the expectations that had come with him from Seattle.

It was typical of Torre, showing loyalty to a struggling player. Nelson was grateful. He responded with a strong ninth, saying, "I was so full of adrenaline it was unbelievable."

And who knows what it did for his psyche? After pitching so poorly all season, Nelson would find himself and come up big in the American League play-offs, rewarding Torre for his faith.

When it was over, the Yankees celebrated on the field, but they had to wait until after the doubleheader's nightcap to break out the champagne. Nevertheless, the party was no less spirited, as the emotions of the long summer spilled all over the clubhouse, much like the bubbly. No one was more emotional than Torre, tears filling his eyes. He couldn't help thinking of his brother Rocco, of his own wife's September observation that he had yet to grieve for his brother.

"She's probably right," Torre said one day.

There hadn't been time with the stress of a pennant race. It hit him now, hit him hard. But only in passing. There still wasn't time. The postseason loomed.

Bernie Williams

11

Home with the Rangers

Joe Torre lit up another fresh cigar, which was always his best friend during a dilemma. In the five days since the Yankees had clinched the East, he'd been wondering who would pitch game one of the division series against the Rangers.

If the choice were made just by the numbers, then Torre knew there was no choice: it would have to be Andy Pettitte, who not only led the American League with those twenty-one wins but proved just how clutch he was by posting thirteen of those wins after a Yankee loss.

What was it about Pettitte that appealed to Torre? The manager pulled hard on his cigar, exhaling slowly. That was easy: it was Pettitte's icy exterior, a zero-anxiety personality. In fact, nothing about his demeanor suggested he'd panic in front of the Rangers, who had held on to win the Western Division despite a furious eleventh-hour finish by the Mariners.

Torre privately wished the Yankees could have been seeded against Cleveland, since his team was a perfect 6-0 at Jacobs Field in 1996 and no one believed the Indians were as fearsome as they had been in 1995. Instead, the Yankees were looking at games three, four, and five of the first round at The Ballpark in Arlington, which was only slightly more acceptable than spending a week at the Kingdome.

The Ballpark was a visual freak show, an amalgam of Camden Yards' homeyness, Tiger Stadium's overhang in right-center, and, in center field, the corporate look of Toronto's SkyDome. For years, the Yankees had been manhandled in Texas: they were 1-5 in 1996 and an appalling 8-34 since 1989. Why? The '96 Rangers were a very good but hardly spectacular team. Yet the Yankees were just as wary of Juan Gonzalez as Edgar Martinez and well aware that Texas played the best defense in the American League.

Obviously, Torre wanted to win games one and two in Yankee Stadium. In fact, he felt he had to. Which is what finally moved him to bypass Pettitte in the opener and hand the ball to David Cone. The manager knew it was an unorthodox move, since Cone had failed to clone that September 2 magic against the A's in his final four starts. In twenty-five subsequent innings, Cone had allowed fourteen earned runs.

Still, Torre called Cone into his office and told him he was the Yankees' best hope for game one. "I need your experience, David," Torre said. That was a constant in the manager's universe, the ability to draw on past experience to survive a crisis. All Cone had to do, Torre said, was treat this October like the others in his past.

Cone nodded, happy to accept such a huge responsibility. But he was disturbed by his lack of consistency in September. "One inning my fastball has been there, then it's gone," Cone said in a private moment. "The only thing I can figure is that it's been a strange summer for my arm. I've never gone through something like this in my life."

His premonition about game one turned out to be true. Only it wasn't just Cone's fastball that deserted him. On good days, Cone's slider looks like a fastball for its first fifty-eight feet to the plate. Then suddenly, without warning, after a hitter has already begun his swing, the ball breaks so sharply it's almost a guarantee that a ground ball will follow.

Arm up, snap the wrist late and hard, follow through. That's the recipe for a slider, and Cone had thrown so many pretty ones since 1987 he became known for what baseball insiders call "perfect muscle-memory."

But for the first time in his career, Cone felt as if his arm had "completely locked up." He couldn't get on top of the slider, couldn't make it travel on a downward plane. Cone was stunned: his best pitch had suddenly evaporated, and the Rangers pounded him for five runs, including two-run homers by Juan Gonzalez and Dean Palmer, en route to a 6–2 win.

He admitted later, "It freaked me out because nothing like that had ever happened to me before. I was sitting in the dugout afterwards, asking myself, 'What happened?' All of a sudden, my arm locks up on me, and there was nothing I could do about it. I mean, I'd never hung that many sliders in one inning. It was kind of scary because I can't understand why it happened in the first place."

The Yankees were in trouble, and, once again, they found themselves leaning on Pettitte. It was Pettitte against Ken Hill, but really the key match-up became Pettitte against Pettitte. Although Torre was right that Pettitte was a master of cool on the mound, he had nevertheless been through a professional crisis in July. For the first time in his career, Pettitte had experienced arm problems and, in his words, "I just didn't know how to deal with it."

Actually, the injury was a mild inflammation in the ligaments, no doubt the result of squeezing something extra out of the cut-fastball. Until now Pettitte had enjoyed the freedom that comes with a healthy arm. He could pick up a ball at any time without pain, never have to worry about the day-after ramifications of playing catch, and never once experience the dread of that first-thing-in-the-morning ritual, which was checking to see how his arm felt.

Cone would often say, "The minute I get out of bed in the morning, I always windmill my arm, just to see how it feels. You never know if it's going to be one of those bad days." Cone's former Met teammate John Franco would say, "The average fan doesn't know how much pain a pitcher lives with day in and day out. The older you get, the closer you have to start your game of catch. I'm at about five feet right now before my arm gets loose."

Of course, there were plenty of remedies available to Pettitte: aspirin was the first line of defense, followed by anti-inflammatory medications like Naprosyn and Indocin. But those had powerful side effects, often causing nausea and diarrhea unless taken with a full meal. And even then there was no guarantee a pitcher wouldn't go to the mound feeling sick. The best remedy of all, obviously, was rest, but that wasn't about to happen. All Pettitte could do was live with the pain.

It wasn't easy. In fact, the normally easygoing Pettitte started to become irritable to the press, to friends, even to his own wife. "Basically, the thing was driving me crazy," he said. But Mel Stottlemyre allowed Pettitte to cheat a little on his delivery, lowering his release point from straight-over-the-top to three-quarters, thereby taking pressure off the elbow. By August, Pettitte was feeling better and even resumed his between-starts workouts.

That's why the Yankees felt so confident in game two: Pettitte had survived the midsummer crisis in his elbow. But against the Rangers, Pettitte suffered an uncharacteristic breakdown in his composure. He overprepared during the week, overthought his batter-by-batter confrontations, and believed that, just because it was October, his cut-fastball had to be better than it had been during his twenty-one-win season.

"I let the whole thing get to me. I don't why, but all of a sudden I stopped having fun out there," Pettitte said. The results were nearly devastating. Juan Gonzalez hit two home runs in his first two at-bats, and the Rangers were ahead, 4–1, after just three innings.

But Pettitte settled down and the Yankees found a savior in Cecil Fielder. Big Daddy had something to prove after a late-season slump had caused Joe Torre to bench him for the first game of the Series in favor of Darryl Strawberry.

Fielder had his flaws as a hitter: he could be beaten with a ninety-plus fastball, especially high in the strike zone, and his long swing wasn't helped by the added flesh on his arms. But Fielder had a remarkable ability to hit a mistake-pitch four hundred feet, and he was also able to cut back on his swing with two strikes. In fact, there were times when Fielder could be the world's biggest, most imposing-looking singles hitter.

The Rangers saw both sides of Fielder in game two. He homered off Ken Hill in the fourth inning, then tied the game in the eighth inning with an opposite-field single off reliever Jeff Russell. And then in the twelfth inning the Yankees discovered one more miracle: the near perfect Rangers defense choked.

With Derek Jeter on second and Tim Raines on first with no one out, Charlie Hayes put down a routine bunt toward third. Dean Palmer picked up the ball and inexplicably threw it past second baseman Mark McLemore, who was covering first. For a moment, the sold-out crowd had trouble believing what it had just seen. Jeter was crossing the plate with a game-winning gift run, and as the Yankees mobbed each other in a crush of high-fives, the Rangers walked off the field with their eyes fixed firmly on their shoelaces. Perhaps they already knew their season was doomed.

The '96 Yankees were a manager's dream, a fact that Joe Torre had pointed out regularly down the stretch. They showed up on time, played hard, didn't complain about lineup decisions, and for the most part kept the nightlife to a minimum. But their benign personality begged the question of whether they were tough enough to handle October pressure.

At times even Willie Randolph, their third-base coach and a link to the more raucous championship teams of the late seventies, seemed to wonder. There were days he wanted to see the Yankees play with a little more fire, even a chip on their shoulder.

Like many former players, Randolph lamented the fraternization in the game today, the friendliness among opposing players. Randolph still doesn't speak to Hal McRae, the one-time Kansas City Royal who wiped him out with a vicious body block at second base during the 1977 ALCS. Randolph thought the play was dirty but he doesn't begrudge McRae.

"That's the way we played in those days," Randolph says. "Those two teams, especially, we really went at each other."

Randolph had been heartened when Tim Raines broke up a double play in Detroit a few weeks earlier with a crushing take-out slide, allowing a go-ahead run to score. He wanted to see the Yankees play with a harder edge, and thought it might be vital in the play-offs.

"I'd like this team to be little more like the teams I played on in the seventies," Randolph said one day during the season. "Those teams were always ready to scrap."

Times had changed, Randolph realized, but as the Yankees headed for Texas he was shocked to find out that those days of constant turmoil weren't necessarily dead. After game two, Reggie Jackson and George Steinbrenner came close to blows on the chartered bus taking the Yankees to Newark Airport for the flight to Dallas. The Yankee crowd outside the stadium was wildly cheering Jackson as he walked the fifty feet from the players' exit to the waiting bus. Chants of "REG-GIE, REG-GIE" filled the air, and Steinbrenner didn't care for it.

"What are you doing here? Who said you could travel with the team?" Steinbrenner snapped as Jackson boarded the bus. "Before you go anywhere, you report to me, you understand?"

All year Jackson had complained that Steinbrenner had failed to recognize his contributions to the Yankees and, furthermore, never promoted him to a position higher than special assistant because, in the words of a friend, "he was just jealous. If Reggie ever became a general manager or vice president, it would be Reggie's team, not George's. And George couldn't live with that."

Jackson had contained his anger for months, until this moment. To hear Steinbrenner speak to him in this way, and in front of several staff members who were already on the bus, was more than his ego could allow. So, finally, Reggie fired back.

"Who the fuck do you think you're talking to?" he said. "I'm tired of your bullshit."

"What did I ever do to you?" said a startled Steinbrenner.

"You treat me like an animal and I'm not going to take it. You hear that? I'm not going to take it anymore."

Jackson had moved to within inches of Steinbrenner, clearly violating his airspace. Although it's highly unlikely Jackson would ever have actually taken a swing at the Yankee owner, Joe Torre nevertheless interceded, gently moving Reggie to the back of the bus. Steinbrenner was apparently so shaken by the incident that he left Texas before the end of the division series, hardly saying another word to Reggie the entire weekend.

Steinbrenner also wanted to avoid facing the Yankee wives on a return flight from Texas, after having prohibited them from accompanying their husbands on the first leg of the trip. So George wasn't around as the Yankees proceeded to finish off the Rangers.

The turning point proved to be the ninth inning of game three, as the Yankees staged a second straight comeback, this time after lefty Darren Oliver had handcuffed them for eight innings. Oliver took a 2–1 lead into the final inning, but gave up singles to Derek Jeter and Tim Raines, putting runners at first and third with no outs.

Rangers manager Johnny Oates then went reluctantly to his bull pen, his club's weakest link. Mike Henneman quickly gave up a sacrifice fly to Bernie Williams, and Raines moved to second on Cecil Fielder's slow-rolling ground out to third. Oates then ordered Henneman to walk Tino Martinez intentionally, bringing up Mariano Duncan. Oates liked the matchup, but Duncan was just the player that Torre and the Yankees wanted to see up in such an important situation.

Signed as a free agent after Randy Velarde departed for the Angels, Duncan was considered a utility man, but when injuries to Tony Fernandez and Pat Kelly pushed him into the job of starting second baseman, he had responded with a career year, hitting .340, 78 points higher than his lifetime average. All year he came up with clutch hits, and his passion for the game, as well as his lively personality, made him a leader in the clubhouse.

In fact, it was Duncan who coined the phrase that became the team motto: "We play today, we win today . . . Dassit." "Dassit" was supposed to mean "That's it," but Duncan wasn't above laughing at his own thick Dominican accent. The credo represented the Yankees' uncomplicated, selfless approach to baseball in the summer of '96. Play and win. Play and win.

Duncan's intensity fueled the Yankees, even if it meant bruising feelings occasionally. His fierce desire nearly erupted into a clubhouse fight one day in Detroit in September when he went face-to-face with Joe Girardi after a win.

That afternoon Derek Jeter had been plunked in the back by a fastball from right-hander Jose Lima, and with the Yankees leading 12–3, Duncan felt it was time to retaliate. Ever since the August 28 brawl with the Mariners, the Yankees had been sensitive to the notion that their pitchers failed to protect their hitters. Even though Jeff Nelson was thrown out for hitting Seattle's Joey Cora the inning after that bench-clearing brawl, Duncan still felt Nelson should go after one of the Tigers' hitters in retaliation for Jeter.

But Nelson was handcuffed by home-plate umpire Ken Kaiser, who immediately warned Girardi that Nelson would be suspended "for a long time" if he hit any of the Tigers.

"Tell him not to even come close," Kaiser said. "Go out there and tell him what I said."

Kaiser turned to the Yankee dugout and relayed the exact same message to Joe Torre. Thus, the manager sent Mel Stottlemyre to the mound, where he met Girardi and Nelson. And the verdict was reached: with the Yankees still in a sweaty pennant race, there would be no counterattack.

The inning proceeded without incident. In fact, Nelson struck out the side. But after the game, Duncan was enraged and loudly told Nelson it was "bullshit" that Lima had gotten away with his crime against Jeter.

"We can't let them do that to us!" Duncan said, prompting Girardi to intercede on Nelson's behalf. Girardi, a graduate of Northwestern University, is one of the game's most well-spoken and thoughtful players. In fact, many Yankees think Girardi is already ready to manage in the big leagues. So when he tried to cope with Duncan's understandable anger, Girardi drew on his power of reason.

"Dunc, Kaiser wouldn't let Nellie go after anyone," Girardi said. "He was going to throw him out of the game, and we can't afford to lose anyone at this point in the season."

Duncan, however, wasn't in the mood to be reasoned with. Indeed, he felt Girardi was dismissing him and taking the umpire's side. He became so angry that, according to several players who witnessed the incident, he and Girardi were soon in each other's faces and had to be separated by coach Don Zimmer. But both players seemed to forget the incident quickly, and now Girardi was rooting hard for Duncan to come through for the Yankees.

Duncan made up his mind to look for Henneman's split-finger fastball, which the Rangers' reliever served up immediately. Duncan lined a single to center, the game winner, as the Yankees moved to within nine innings of finishing off the Rangers.

The Yankees were hoping Kenny Rogers could end the series in game four, but Torre knew that was a long shot. First, Rogers had been suffering with an on-again, off-again inflammation in his shoulder throughout the season's second half. And no one knew how Rogers would stand up to the psychological weight of the play-offs, especially against his former teammates, whom he had so casually insulted during spring training. No one in Texas had forgotten that Rogers said he chose the Yankees because he "wanted to play with a team that had a chance to win."

Rogers said he had no regrets in uttering those words, but now they were coming back to haunt him. The Rangers hit him hard, and Torre pulled him in the third inning, trailing 2–0. The lead grew to 4–0 as Juan Gonzalez hit his fifth home run of the series, off of Brian Boehringer. But Bernie Williams led a third straight Yankee comeback, hitting two home runs, one off starter Bobby Witt, and then his second against Mike Stanton.

Williams, a switch-hitter, had gone deep from both sides of the plate, testimony to just how far he'd come as a full-fledged star. Williams had arrived in the Yankee organization as a shy, extremely nervous rookie in 1991 and was immediately ridiculed by superhip Yankees like Mel Hall. Williams was sure an easy target: after all, he was college-educated, working toward a degree in biology, and played classical guitar as a hobby.

When Williams walked around the room in his reading glasses, he hardly seemed like a classic Yankee power hitter. But he rose fast to become one of the game's most dominant threats, turning down the Yankees' multiyear offer of $4 million a year, demanding Ken Griffey–type money of $7 million per. Williams defeated the Yankees in arbitration for $3 million in 1996, and, after hitting .305 with twenty-nine home runs and 102 RBIs, was close to the American League elite.

Williams succeeded in a year with near tragedy as well. His son, Bernie, was suffering from a bone infection behind his left ear when the Yankees were in Detroit in early June, and an emergency phone call to the clubhouse almost shattered his world.

Williams was talking to a group of reporters when Yankee traveling secretary David Szen broke through the crowd and said, "Bernie, it's for you. It's your wife." Williams was in the middle of a sentence when Szen added, "Bernie, it's an emergency."

Williams broke away, took the call, and, for the next five minutes, listened in shock: the infection had not responded to antibiotics, and now doctors had no choice but to insert a tube into the mastoid bone and aggressively remove the fluids. It was a dangerous procedure, and Williams was told to fly to Puerto Rico immediately.

The outfielder barely had time for a shower before jumping into a cab to the airport. Williams flew to Miami but wouldn't be able to reach San Juan until the following morning. That night, he said, "was the worst of my life." He was unable to reach his wife and family, since they'd camped out at the hospital and the switchboard had already closed down.

"Finally, I just closed my eyes, lay down on the bed, and waited for the hours to pass," Williams said. The morning came, and Williams, consumed with fear and worry, finally boarded the first flight to Puerto Rico. Later that day, doctors successfully removed the infection from the younger Williams's head. The boy's life had been saved.

So maybe it was fitting that the final run of the final game of the division series was produced by Williams. After that long home run off Stanton, he paused a moment before circling the bases. There was a reason for that, and it had nothing to do with the Yankees' 6–4 lead, which was about to propel them into the championship series with the Orioles.

"That home run was for my son," Williams said. All around him champagne was flying and the clubhouse music was at full blast. You had to listen closely as Williams, his eyes moistening, said, "That one was for Bernie."

12

Orioles-Yankees, the Final Act

T he fly ball didn't look like much when it left the bat in the seventh inning of game one against the Orioles, but 1996 had long since taught fans not to underestimate the flight of a juiced ball, no matter how routine it appeared. Likewise, the player who hit it had long since taught them not to underestimate Derek Jeter.

The baseball season had begun in New York with a great debate about the two rookie shortstops in town. Rey Ordonez announced his arrival with a spectacular relay throw from his knees at Shea Stadium, and Derek Jeter responded the next day with an exceptional over-the-shoulder catch of a blooper in Cleveland.

By midseason Ordonez led the world in TV highlights, a nightly performer on ESPN's SportsCenter, while Jeter more quietly made all the plays and went about learning to hit in the big leagues. By the season's end there was no debate. The

Jimmy Key

test of will that 162 games provides had separated the two phenoms: the dog days brought out the rookie in Ordonez as he made too many careless errors for the Mets and faded with the bat, while Jeter thrived in the heat of a pennant race, slowly but surely growing day by day with both the glove and the bat.

It is supposed to be suicide to try to win a championship with a rookie shortstop, relying on a kid to make the plays at the toughest position in the game. But the Yankees came to learn quickly that Jeter, who turned twenty-two in June, was no kid.

"He's unusual," Willie Randolph said one day during the summer. "He reminds me a lot of a young Don Mattingly. You can tell by the way a guy carries himself—like he belongs."

He was the sixth pick in the 1992 June draft, the first high school player selected that year. The Yankees loved his bat, his athleticism, and the uncommon cool he displayed for his high school team in Kalamazoo, Michigan. They weren't sure if he'd make it as a shortstop in the big leagues, and doubts remained even as he zoomed through the farm system, chewing up minor-league pitching. He made too many throwing errors, and his footwork was clumsy at times, even at Columbus in 1995.

But Gene Michael, a former shortstop himself, believed in him and convinced George Steinbrenner that Jeter should be the shortstop in 1996. The Yankees had Tony Fernandez under contract for '96, but Joe Torre declared Jeter his shortstop during the winter so there would be no great debate in spring training. Torre tried to deflect the pressure on Jeter by saying that if he hit .250, that would be fine, "as long as he makes the plays defensively."

Coaches Randolph and Don Zimmer worked with Jeter endlessly in Tampa on his defense, his footwork, and it began to show. The rest was Jeter; he had savvy, an ability to make the big play that couldn't be taught. He didn't say much, but he had a presence that allowed him to fit in easily among the veterans. Teammates sensed immediately the kid was there to stay.

"Two weeks into spring training I knew he'd be fine," Mariano Duncan, the twelve-year veteran second baseman, said during the season. "Even then it was like he'd been in the big leagues five years."

By October no one was suprised when Jeter climbed to a still higher level. He'd started game-winning rallies during the darkest moments of the Rangers series, in the late innings of game two and three, and hit .415.

And now, in game one against the Orioles—delayed a day by rain—with the Yankees trailing 3–2 and his teammates pleading for him to "Stay hot, kid," Jeter appeared to be beaten on a ninety-four-mph fastball by Armando Benitez. But he had an uncanny way of pulling his hands in tight as he swung and inside-outing the ball to the opposite field with some sting.

This time he got enough of it to bring the crowd to its feet, even if it didn't look anything like a home-run swing. With the short porch in right, and the knowledge that worse-looking swings had produced home runs all around the majors this year, fans sensed that anything was possible.

How right they were, too, but only because a twelve-year-old kid named Jeffrey Maier reached out from the stands and got his own glove on the ball.

"It was like magic," Orioles outfielder Tony Tarasco would say. "I was about to catch the ball, and it disappeared."

The crowd erupted when umpire Richie Garcia signaled home run, twirling his right index finger in a circle above his head. As Tarasco and then other Orioles descended in fury upon Garcia, reporters were already dashing from the press box through the stadium corridors toward right field.

By any definition, the kid was a big story, a fan who altered the outcome of a play-off game. In New York, where each local paper had several writers in search of fresh angles for a story, the kid became an instant celebrity. Soon everyone knew Jeffrey Maier was a seventh grader from Old Tappan, New Jersey, a Yankee fan who became the toast of his neighborhood for helping the Yankees steal a win.

But with celebrity came controversy. Columnists and radio voices accused the media and Maier's own family of sending the wrong message, because interfering with the game was wrong and technically grounds for ejection from the stadium. It was one thing, the critics screamed, to put the kid's picture on the front page of the newspapers and interview him on national TV, but it was another for his family to shepherd him around to the morning TV shows the next day and then take up the New York *Daily News* on its offer to bring him to game two in a limo and sit him in box seats behind the dugout.

The criticism became so strong that the kid's father wound up going on WFAN to defend his family in a rancorous interview with Mike Francesa and Chris Russo.

But there was no debating the impact of his act. The home run stood, despite the Orioles' vehement arguments, and the game was tied 3–3.

There was nothing lucky about Bernie Williams's monster home run to left off Randy Myers four innings later that won the game, but the Orioles were understandably bitter afterward. Minutes after the game, they were gathered around a portable VCR unit, watching the play on tape over and over, each replay accompanied by their own profane commentary.

"We got screwed, completely fucking screwed," came an angry voice from the crowd of players.

Meanwhile, on the clubhouse TV, not more than ten feet above the VCR monitor, the feed from the postgame interview room was being shown. There was Garcia, admitting, after seeing a replay himself, that he'd made a bad call, while still insisting the ball would not have been caught.

"That's where you all ought to be," Eddie Murray growled to reporters as he pointed toward Garcia. "That's where the fuckin' game was won."

Orioles owner Peter Angelos, at the same time, was already on the phone with club lawyers, trying to determine what course of action could be taken. Davey Johnson, after being ejected, had told the umpires he was playing the game under protest, but to Davey this was merely an official way of making sure the world knew the Orioles got screwed. The rule book says that judgment calls aren't subject to protest.

Angelos didn't care. He wanted justice, the same as George Steinbrenner would have if the play had happened against the Yankees. Angelos used reams of paper filing the protest—based not on the call but on Garcia's admission of error—and then distributed a pile of six-page explanations of the protest to the press.

No one took it very seriously. The Yankees had gotten a break, and nothing was going to change it. The official rejection came two days later, but by then the Birds were back in the series, having gained the split they were looking for at the stadium by beating the Yankees 5–4 in game two.

And while their bitterness would linger, it was Steinbrenner whose mood had turned sour. Their good fortune aside, the Yankees hadn't hit much at all in the two games, and suddenly there was a feeling that their season-long dominance of the Orioles was gone as the series now moved to Baltimore for three games.

"Just watch," Steinbrenner said bitterly, as his top baseball people gathered in his office after game two. "We're gonna go down there and get swept. They've got Eddie Murray in their lineup, and we've got Cecil Fielder and Charlie Hayes."

It was a not-so-subtle slap at the trades Bob Watson had engineered—with The Boss's approval, of course—during the season, but by now it barely fazed the general manager.

George always had to have someone to blame when things went wrong, and in 1996 it was almost always Watson.

Camden Yards was an intimidating place for many a visiting team in 1996. Charming as it is, with its new/old feel, the ballpark is a joke to pitchers. The dimensions everywhere are short by major-league standards, and Orioles pitchers insist privately that the fences are even closer than what is marked. The stadium was built with home runs in mind, and the '96 Orioles hit more dingers than any team in history.

Yet the Yankees were already 6-0 against them as the teams lined up for game three. Maybe it was no coincidence, either. The place was a graveyard for mediocre pitching, of which the Orioles had had plenty during the season. No team in the league, on the other hand, made fewer mistake-pitches than the Yankees. Their total of 143 home runs allowed during the '96 season was by far the lowest in the American League, which simply meant they were better equipped to survive the Baltimore bandbox.

Though it didn't look that way when Todd Zeile hammered Jimmy Key's first-inning curveball into the left-field seats for a 2–0 Oriole lead. Yankee fans had to be squirming at that moment. If Key didn't have his precision control and command, the game could get ugly in a hurry.

But if anyone could handle the jolt of falling behind before he'd even gotten an out, it was Key. No one was more widely admired by his teammates for his professionalism, his poise, and his ability to deliver in the clutch.

No less a pitcher than David Cone has said more than once, "There's nobody I'd rather see out there in a big game than Jimmy Key."

Key had come to the Yankees as a free agent immediately after helping the Blue Jays win a World Series in 1992, and during his first two years in pinstripes he'd become the emotional soul of the ball club, along with Don Mattingly. He was so good, so reliable every fifth day, that he gave the Yankees the kind of aura Roger Clemens gave the Red Sox in the eighties.

The loss of Key to shoulder surgery in '95 had been a crippling blow, and he was just 12-11 in '96 after amazing the entire organization by being ready in April. He'd absorbed some humiliating defeats as he navigated the peaks and valleys of postsurgical pitching. And twice he'd been forced to go on the disabled list, in May and June, but for Key it was a necessary evil.

"I'm doing all this so I can be ready in September," he said early in the season. "That's my goal."

He was, too. He hadn't lost since August 21, and he'd pitched well in his one start against the Rangers. Now he seemed to be in trouble after Brady Anderson's single and Zeile's home run. He still didn't have an out. And all he did was proceed to throw eight innings of brilliance, giving up a second-inning single to B. J. Surhoff and then nothing else.

After the game Joe Torre would shake his head in wonder. It had been just fourteen months earlier that Torre, recently fired by the Cardinals, and Key, weeks removed from surgery, wound up working together as broadcasters at the Little League World Series in Williamsport, Pennsylvania. Now here was Key, perhaps pitching Torre to the big-league World Series that had eluded him his entire career.

"He's a remarkable human being," Torre said. "Considering his age [thirty-five], what he went through with the surgery, and how much we needed him, to do what he did tonight is just phenomenal."

Given the circumstances, it may have been the single greatest performance of the season to that point by any Yankee, and yet Key's heroics were overshadowed by the drama of still another late-inning comeback.

Davey Johnson would single out the top of the eighth inning as the pivotal moment in the entire series. Mike Mussina was at his best, his knuckle-curve nasty all night and his fastball nipping the corners.

"He was going so good," Johnson would say at the series' end, "I was sure he was going to finish."

Leading 2–1, Mussina was four outs away, without a hint of trouble, when the Yankees struck again. Jeter doubled to the opposite field. Mussina hung a curve to Bernie Williams, who singled home Jeter to tie the score. Tino Martinez then lined a double down the left-field line, setting up the most bizarre play of the series. After the relay the ball simply slipped out of Zeile's hand as he pump-faked toward second, allowing Williams to jump up from a slide and score just ahead of Cal Ripken's throw to give the Yankees a 3–2 lead.

Finally, Mussina, who would admit afterward to being rattled by the Zeile play, hung a curve to Fielder, and Big Daddy said thank you, parking it in the left-field seats. It was 5–2, and, perhaps at that moment, both teams sensed the inevitable.

The Yankees had now rallied dramatically in each of their five play-off wins, and for the seventh straight time in Camden Yards, they had been better than the Orioles in the late innings.

"This is a remarkable run we're on," said Torre that night. "We played so many one- and two-run games this year, close games don't bother us."

John Wetteland finished up to earn the save, his eighth against the Orioles in 1996. But the win, and the night, belonged to Key. Afterward he was as stoic as ever, but proud, too. "It means a lot to me," he said. "It tells me that all the work paid off, that I'm back to being the pitcher I was before the surgery."

Predictably, game four was messier, with Kenny Rogers and Rocky Coppinger doing the honors on the mound. Given another opportunity because the rain that pushed game one back a day had eliminated the travel day and prevented Andy Pettitte from coming back on three days' rest, Rogers again failed miserably.

The Yankees gave him a 5–2 lead, yet he couldn't get out of the fourth inning. But once again the bull pen came to the rescue. David Weathers, the right-hander who had looked like such a bust after the July 31 trade for Mark Hutton, took the game to Mariano Rivera and John Wetteland.

Meanwhile, the Yankees further destroyed the Orioles psychologically, beating them at their own game this time by lighting up the joint with four home runs. Darryl Strawberry hit two, and Paul O'Neill and Bernie Williams hit one each.

Finally, Rivera broke whatever Oriole spirit remained. Ahead 8–4 after Strawberry's second home run, Rivera gave up three straight singles in the bottom of the eighth as the Birds loaded the bases with no outs.

As superhuman as Rivera had been throughout the season, the Orioles were the one team that had made him look ordinary, hitting him hard on two different occasions. But now, after raising their hopes, he drove a stake through their heart, turning the dial up on his fastball to strike out Chris Hoiles and Brady Anderson and getting Zeile to pop out, ending the inning.

"What else can the guy do this year?" David Cone wondered aloud about Rivera afterward.

The win put the Yankees ahead 3–1 and triggered a sense of inevitability about the series in both clubhouses.

"We've played them so tough," said Rafael Palmeiro. "But we just can't seem to do what it takes to beat them."

The hours before game five seemed to be little more than Yankee preparation for the World Series. Looking ahead, the media mobbed Torre and Watson in the dugout before the game. Each of them held court for a half-hour. And while they stood not more than twenty feet apart, they may as well have been in different worlds.

Watson still couldn't allow himself to enjoy the proceedings, consumed, it seemed, by his private war with George Steinbrenner. The Boss had made a show late in the season of saying Torre would be back for the second year of his contract no matter how the Yankees finished, but he had pointedly refused to address Watson's job status at the time.

Watson had continued to talk about the possibility he would be fired, even as the ball club was celebrating its division-clinching win all around him in September. He seemed no more at ease now, answering questions stiffly as the media gathered around him. He offered a sense of resentment of Steinbrenner, too, Watson being a former player forced to answer constantly to a man who knew relatively little about the intricacies of the game.

He was asked by a Houston writer how working for Steinbrenner was different from working for Drayton McLane, the Astros owner, who was also notorious for meddling.

"George has been in the game a whole lot longer," said Watson. "When it comes to baseball, Drayton only knows if his team won or lost and what the attendance was. George knows what's in the box score. He knows what an ERA is."

It was a good line, but Watson didn't so much as smile. Finally, he was asked if he even wanted to come back for another year with Steinbrenner.

"I signed on for two years," he said solemnly. "Plus an option."

"I don't think that's the answer we were looking for," a writer said lightheartedly, trying to get a chuckle from Watson.

"That's the answer you got," Watson responded.

This was in stark contrast to the warmth of the nearby Torre session. The manager's quest for the World Series, coupled with his family problems, had become the most compelling story of the postseason, and the national media were trying to catch up on a story that was already familiar in New York.

So Torre was being asked to paint a family portrait in the dugout. His father had been a New York City cop, he explained. There were two brothers, two sisters, and Joe was the youngest by eight and a half years.

"I was the baby of the family," Torre said. "I had a lot of parents. I was supposed to be a doctor. Then a priest. I took a little of each and played baseball. My sister became a nun when I was ten or eleven years old. When she left home, she gave me a glove and told me to say an 'Our Father' every time I used it. My family has been my life."

It didn't take long for Torre and his family to become the focus of NBC's telecast, either. The Yankees jumped out to a 6–0 lead against Scott Erickson, as Jim Leyritz, Cecil Fielder, and Darryl Strawberry all hit third-inning home runs, and any remaining suspense was gone.

So NBC broadcaster Bob Costas began to detail Torre's year of mixed emotions: the death of his oldest brother, Rocco, from a heart attack during the season, and the ongoing ordeal of his other brother, Frank, who had been waiting eleven weeks for a heart transplant in Columbia Presbyterian Medical Center. Costas told the story of how Frank, a member of the Milwaukee Braves' World Series teams in 1957 and '58, had given little brother Joe his '58 ring, a ring that was stolen out of Joe's New York hotel room in 1972. Now, all these years later, Joe wanted a ring he could give to Frank's son as a kind of repayment.

All this made Torre's quest a little more poignant. By the end of the game, when John Wetteland got Cal Ripken to ground out for the final out in a 6–4 victory, a national TV audience understood the emotion pouring out of Torre as he cried while standing on the top step of the dugout, watching his team celebrate on the field. He hugged his coaches, then each of his players as they came off the field and made their way into the clubhouse.

"I was trying to keep my emotions in check for the last five innings," Torre said. "It was hard not to think about all the years of waiting and what it meant to my family. So many people wanted this for me."

The pictures of Torre seemed to touch people everywhere. He would be surprised to arrive home that night and find twenty congratulatory messages on his answering machine; he would be shocked to hear at least half of the well-wishers crying themselves during their message. And the messages kept coming all week.

"I had no idea so many people would be so moved," Torre said later.

Even Torre's third wife, Alice, married to Joe since 1987, was taken aback by the emotion she saw from her husband that day.

"When I saw him crying in Baltimore," Alice later told Tom Verducci of *Sports Illustrated*, "it just blew me away. I know how much it meant to him. I've never seen him cry like that. That's when I could really tell what it meant to him."

The locker-room scene Torre shared with his family was equally touching. Such extremes. At the trophy presentation Torre dedicated the win to his brothers, one dead and the other waiting for a medical miracle. He could barely get the words out on national TV as his emotion overwhelmed him again. Then, minutes later, he was kissing his wife, hugging his two sisters, and cuddling his nine-month-old daughter.

Soon he excused himself. He had a phone call to make. Brother Frank was waiting to hear from him in the hospital.

Down the hall there was none of the despair that was so evident in the Orioles' clubhouse after games three and four. The Baltimore players seemed almost relieved they would no longer have to explain why they couldn't beat the Yankees in their own ballpark.

Not that it was so tough to figure out. The Yankees were more well rounded and had better pitching. Indeed, in a year of unprecedented offense, pitching once again prevailed. The team whose pitchers surrendered the fewest home runs in the league outdueled the team whose hitters hit the most home runs in history.

"We were a one-dimensional team," Davey Johnson said. "If you make a mistake, our guys hit it out. But the Yankee pitchers didn't make many mistakes."

But that explanation was perhaps too simple after the different paths the two teams took all season. As much turmoil as the Orioles had overcome in earning a wild-card berth and shocking the Cleveland Indians in the first round of the play-offs, in the end they were still missing that special something the Yankees had in 1996. And finally they could admit it.

"I think we had better players than the Yankees," Assistant General Manager Kevin Malone said after the final game. "But they had the better team. Their whole approach to the game was just more determined. We had a group of superstars, while the Yankees kept coming and grinding and pressing. They were more blue-collar. We're a little white-collar. We have to change the makeup here."

It was perhaps the ultimate commentary on the yearlong rivalry. Both teams had spent and spent and spent in an effort to win a championship. The irony was that after all the off-season maneuvering and padding of the payrolls, it wasn't the imports that made the difference but the Yankees' homegrown talent—Jeter, Williams, Pettitte, and Super Mariano Rivera.

That was a tribute to former general manager Gene Michael, who had followed through on his vow to end the years of trading young talent for stopgap veterans. Buck Showalter deserved credit as well for establishing a team-oriented atmosphere that eased the transition to a new manager. But there was no denying that Steinbrenner had pulled off his power play, managing to put together an admirable, winning team. The combination of payroll, team chemistry, and the perfect manager for this particular ball club had produced magic.

"A team like this is a rarity," Torre said that day. "This team wasn't concerned about numbers, only winning. We used all the ingredients—that's what glued us together."

Whatever the differences between the Orioles and the Yankees, they made for a compelling rivalry. And on this day Peter Angelos pledged to make it even tougher on the Yankees next year.

"New York won a battle in a war that is ongoing," he said after game five. "As far as the Orioles are concerned, we will continue in our efforts again and again until our pursuit is successful. And it will be. Baltimore will have a winner."

No, the Orioles weren't going away, not with Angelos's deep pockets. But what did the Yankees care? They were going to the World Series.

13

A Classic Fall Classic

Game One . . . October 20 . . . Braves 12, Yankees 1

The Yankees found out what it meant to be a National League team, no match for a machine that threw perfect ninety-five-mph fastballs and treated the World Series like batting practice.

In fact, the Yankees weren't just beaten by the Braves in game one. They were overmatched, out-gunned, and even humiliated in the 12–1 loss. Was it possible the Braves were that much better than the Yankees? That John Smoltz could have thrown harder than any American League pitcher the Bombers had seen all year? And that Andy Pettitte, their best pitcher, couldn't even get out of the third inning?

Over and over the Yankees had dismissed the Braves' 32–1 whipping of the Cardinals in games five, six, and seven of the NLCS, insisting their own pitchers were better than anything

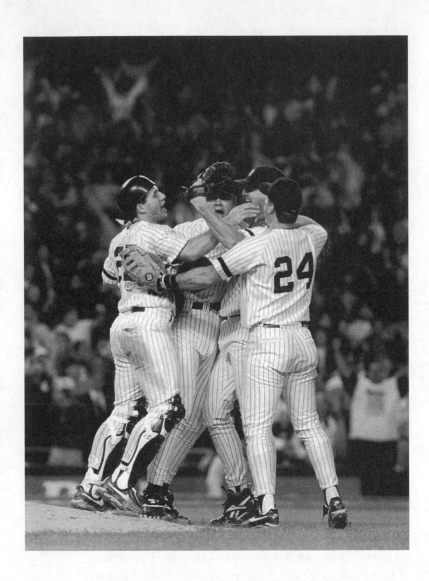

the Braves had seen in October. But Chipper Jones said, "The ball looks like the moon right now," and the Yankees looked just as helpless as the Cardinals.

Andruw Jones, the nineteen-year-old rookie, blasted a two-run home run in the second, then Pettitte collapsed altogether in the third, when the Braves scored six runs. There, up front and in their faces, the Yankees were finding out why the Cardinals had never had a chance after game four.

"It's beyond me what happened out there," a crushed Pettitte said afterward. "I felt fine. I had good stuff, and then the next thing I know the game is out of hand. My job was to keep my team close, and I blew it."

"We ran into a buzz saw. That team is very hot, obviously," said Wade Boggs. "But that's why the World Series is seven games, not one. You don't win a World Championship in just one game. We'll be back [tonight]."

You heard that a lot in the clubhouse afterward, the same lines that bordered on self-delusion: Just one game . . . easy to forget . . . we've bounced back before. But Brian Boehringer, who relieved Pettitte in the third inning, admitted it was "shocking" to see the potential Cy Young Award winner get flogged.

"It was the last thing that any of us could've imagined," Boehringer said. "The way Andy was throwing, it seemed like he would be okay. You never think that Andy would've gotten hit like that."

But the Yankees melted when Andruw Jones took Pettitte deep in the second, crushing a 2-2 fastball that Pettitte said "was just an awful pitch." The worst was yet to come. Jeff Blauser and Marquis Grissom led off with back-to-back singles, after which Mark Lemke bunted both runners over.

That was typical Braves strategy—typical National League chess-work, really. Chipper Jones then punched a two-strike single into left, past the Yankees' drawn-in infield. That was another mistake by Pettitte, a cut-fastball that was left, swollen and vulnerable, over the middle of the plate.

With the Braves' lead 4–0, the Yankees were almost history. Fred McGriff lined an opposite single to left, making it 5–0, and Pettitte was gone after walking Javy Lopez. Joe Torre came to the mound, not so much to take the ball from Pettitte, but to tell him the Yankees would still need him in the Series, and not to let the images of defeat penetrate too deeply.

But the Yankees didn't do much to let Pettitte off the hook. Andruw Jones became only the second player in World Series history to hit two home runs in his first two at-bats, this time beating Boehringer on an awful 3-2 slider, and the Braves cruised behind John Smoltz.

The Yankees could blame the six off days—one last rain-out pushed back game one a day—for their obvious rust, but Derek Jeter said, "Even in the regular season, I'd have to say Smoltz would've beaten us."

For the moment at least, October seemed to belong to the Braves.

Game Two . . . October 21 . . . Braves 4, Yankees 0

The final out came as a relief, because it meant the Yankees could finally be spared another inning of an awful mismatch. No one could touch Greg Maddux. No one could stop Fred McGriff. The Yankees had never looked so feeble.

Was it all ending so quickly? So emptily? Their 4–0 loss in game two represented all that was wrong with the Yankees in the wake of a six-day layoff after the ALCS. The Yankees' best postseason pitcher, Jimmy Key, was beaten by a better one.

And the Yankees' most trustworthy hitters, Derek Jeter and Bernie Williams, were just invisible.

For years, the Yankees had heard about the illusion of Maddux's two-seam fastball. Now they knew. In eight innings, Maddux threw just eighty-two pitches. He got eighteen ground-ball outs, five of which were tapped harmlessly back to him. Eight Yankees were retired on the first pitch. And Andruw Jones was the only Braves outfielder to record a put-out.

"Maddux was just unbelievable," Wade Boggs said in quiet awe. "It's like playing Wiffle ball, he gets so much movement on the ball. He'd throw a pitch right down the middle, you thought you'd put a good swing on it, and then the bottom would fall out."

The Yankees had fallen behind early and barely threatened against Maddux. Only once all night did the Bombers bring the crowd to life, when Jeter and Tim Raines led off the bottom of the sixth with singles.

But it was just another cruel joke perpetrated by Maddux, a four-time Cy Young Award winner. He got Boggs to bounce into a 4–6–3 double play and ended the rally with Williams's soft grounder to second base. The Yankees, already down 4–0, had drawn their last breath.

Maddux called it "a turning point in the game." Suddenly the tension of the World Series was gone and the night got ugly. The game was stopped seven times as fans ran onto the field, then were tackled by security personnel and dragged away for arrest.

All this because Key, although pitching respectably, was no match for Maddux. He allowed four runs and ten hits in six innings, and admitted, "I was in trouble the whole time." Even in the first inning, in a relatively harmless one-run rally, the Braves showed Key they were smarter than the average, swing-for-the-ozone American League hitter.

With Mark Lemke on second and one out, Key left an out-side fastball to McGriff up about chest-high. Instead of trying to power a monster home run into the deliciously close right-field porch, McGriff went with the pitch, lining a single to left-center. Key shook his head. "Freddie sure knows how to hit mistake-pitches," he said later, "and that's what he got. I made mistakes and he took advantage of them."

McGriff did the damage, all right, adding an RBI single in the third and a sacrifice fly in the fifth. By then it was 3–0 and the rest of the night was a personal exhibition for Maddux. Was he the best? Or did the title belong now to Smoltz, the certain Cy Young Award winner this season? Joe Torre smiled sadly. "We've seen pitchers who could really hump it up and throw a great game, but they're not all on one team," he said.

That wasn't defeat in Torre's words, just an acceptance of re-ality. Key, in fact, admitted, "The best thing that happened to the Braves was them being down 3–1 to the Cardinals. All of a sudden they woke up and said, 'Hey, we're about to get beat.' And no one's been able to stop them, including us."

Game Three . . . October 22 . . . Yankees 5, Braves 2

The Yankees arrived at Fulton County Stadium early in the af-ternoon and tried to treat the day as any other: card games, TV, a bite to eat . . . anything to help them forget they were becoming an October joke.

"An embarrassment" is how David Cone put it, which tells you what the Yankees really thought about game two of the World Series. Which is why they turned to Cone and silently pleaded: Help.

Joe Torre did his part, rearranging one-third of his lineup. The slumping Paul O'Neill, Wade Boggs, and Tino Martinez were replaced by Darryl Strawberry, Charlie Hayes, and Cecil Fielder, who had to play first base, since the designated hitter is not used in World Series games hosted by the National League team.

But the only change that really mattered was on the mound. Where the long layoff before the Series had turned the Yankees stale in games one and two as a team, it rejuvenated Cone. Eleven days of rest was exactly what his tired arm needed, and after having tried to finesse his way through starts against the Rangers and Orioles, the zip was back in his fastball.

Cone, in fact, called it easily the best fastball he'd had since his seven no-hit innings against the A's on September 2, the day he returned from his aneurysm surgery. The result this night was six strong innings that included a life-and-death jam in the sixth and finally a 5–2 victory that was aided by another monstrous home run by Bernie Williams.

"It's as big as any game I've pitched," Cone said.

It was Cone, not Tom Glavine, the major league's best big-moment pitcher, who survived the game's biggest crisis. With a 2–0 lead—RBI singles off Glavine by Williams in the first inning, Strawberry in the third—Cone set himself up for trouble by walking Glavine to lead off the sixth.

After Marquis Grissom dropped a single in front of Raines, the Yankees caught a break when Mark Lemke popped out trying to bunt the runners over.

But Cone then walked Chipper Jones to load the bases, creating an instant crisis in the Yankee dugout. Torre already had Graeme Lloyd warming up, and with Fred McGriff standing at the plate, the manager needed answers from Cone, fast.

He went to the mound and, according to Torre, the dialogue went like this:

"David, this is really important; I need to know the truth. Are you okay?"

"I'm fine. I can get McGriff."

"Are you sure?"

"I'm losing my splitter a little bit, but it's more mechanical than anything."

Torre, literally nose-to-nose with Cone, said he then looked his pitcher "right in the eye" and accepted his answers as the truth.

Cone later joked, "I lied. But I was lying to myself, too. Like, 'Yeah, sure, I can get Fred McGriff out with the bases loaded.' "

But it was just the kind of lie Torre wanted to hear.

"I trust David," Torre said. "He had that look in his eyes that I hadn't seen in a while. The thing was, I didn't really want to take him out of there, but I wanted to hear him say it. If he had hesitated, I would have taken him out. But he didn't."

Cone was bold in going after McGriff. Gambling that he would be looking fastball on the first pitch, Cone dropped a very hittable slider in that froze McGriff for a called strike. Having planted that thought, Cone went back to his heater, getting up and in just enough to produce a pop-out to Derek Jeter in shallow center. Glavine might have tagged and scored on the back-pedaling Jeter, but he decided not to try.

Cone then battled Ryan Klesko to a 3-and-2 count, finally throwing a fastball on the inside corner that locked up Klesko. But home-plate umpire Tim Welke judged it to be a shade too high, causing Cone to extend his arms toward the plate in disbelief.

"I really, really wanted that pitch," he said after the game.

Instead, the walk cut the Yankees' lead to 2–1. Then Cone got lucky. After throwing a nasty slider for strike one to Javy Lopez, the Braves' hottest hitter for most of the postseason, he threw a terrible pitch, a hanging slider about shoulder-high. It was so bad that it seemed to fool Lopez, and he took an awkward swing that produced a pop-up to Joe Girardi.

"I got away with one there," Cone said.

The Yankees weren't doing much with Glavine, but one inning later, the National League rules worked to their advantage: Bobby Cox was forced to pinch-hit for his starter.

That brought on Greg McMichael, who represented the soft underbelly of the Braves' mighty pitching staff—mediocre middle relief. They had no Mariano Rivera to bridge the gap between their starters and closer Mark Wohlers, and the Yankees quickly took advantage. Bernie Williams crushed a hanging change-up—McMichael's out pitch—powering it into the right-field seats to give the Yankees a 4–1 lead.

Soon it was 5–1, and suddenly the Braves looked mortal, especially in the late innings. They couldn't go bull pen for bull pen with the Yankees, even on this night, when a jittery Rivera needed to be rescued in the eighth.

Grissom had tripled and Lemke singled. Bang. And bang. The Braves were within reach, at 5–2. Rivera struck out Chipper Jones, but Torre made the bold move of bringing in Graeme Lloyd—yes, Graeme Lloyd!—to pitch to the Braves' powerful lefties, and Lloyd delivered, getting McGriff to fly to center and then striking out Klesko to end the inning.

The image was almost too stunning for the eyes to accept: Lloyd running off the field, accepting high-fives from the Yankees, after taming the Braves in the World Series.

Right then and there the Yankees decided: nothing is impossible.

Game Four . . . October 23 . . . Yankees 8, Braves 6
(Ten Innings)

Mark Wohlers legitimately throws his fastball ninety-eight to ninety-nine mph, and occasionally tops a hundred on the radar gun. Yet Wohlers gave up eight home runs during the '96 season, or seven more than Mariano Rivera, because his long delivery gives hitters a better look at his fastball.

So he likes to keep hitters from cheating on his heater. On this night, when he saw Jim Leyritz take a couple of healthy hacks at fastballs, fouling them off, Wohlers made a fateful decision to throw his slider.

The Braves had already seen a 6–0 lead shrink to 6–3, as the Yankees rallied against Denny Neagle, and now the Bombers were threatening again, with two runners on in the eighth inning.

Leyritz, with a 1-and-2 count, was looking fastball. Against Wohlers, a hitter can't afford to look for anything else.

"But I was ready for the slider," he said. "And he left one out over the plate."

A hanger, fat and juicy. Leyritz didn't miss it, launching it over the wall in left to tie the game 6–6 and leave the Braves dumbfounded. It would turn out to be the defining moment of the Series, indeed the entire Yankee postseason. Their greatest comeback of all, the second-greatest in World Series history. (In 1929 the Philadelphia A's came back from an 8–1 deficit.)

"The momentum is ours now," Tim Raines proclaimed. "Things are going our way."

The Braves, meanwhile, would have a question to ponder all winter: what if Wohlers had thrown his fastball? Or, as one Yankee player privately wondered, "How do you get beat in that situation with your second-best pitch?"

Bobby Cox didn't mince words himself after the game.

"A lot of things went wrong for us," he said. "We just blew the game."

Leyritz's home run only tied the game, but it made the win inevitable. The Yankees had overcome still another horrid start by Kenny Rogers, and it was a rare night in October that they would lose a battle of the bull pens, especially once Wohlers was gone.

Sure enough, they rallied against Steve Avery in the tenth inning. With two outs, Tim Raines drew a four-pitch walk from Avery, who then allowed Derek Jeter a single to right after being ahead 0-2 in the count.

Cox then made a gutsy decision, intentionally walking Bernie Williams, and loading the bases for Andy Fox. Fox had pinch-run for Cecil Fielder in the ninth, when the Yankees strung together three hits but failed to score.

But Joe Torre had saved Wade Boggs for just such a spot, and now he used him to hit for Fox. Boggs fell behind 1-and-2, laid off a borderline breaking ball on the outside corner, and worked the count to 3-and-2. Avery then missed badly with a fastball up and in, and the Yankees went berserk in their dugout as the go-ahead run scored on the bases-loaded walk.

Cox could only lower his head in despair. He called for Brad Clontz to face Charlie Hayes, but by this time it seemed nothing could go wrong for the Yankees. Hayes, jammed by Clontz's fastball, lifted an easy humpback liner to Ryan Klesko at first.

Somehow Klesko lost the ball in the lights, giving the Yankees another run and an 8–6 lead. That allowed Graeme Lloyd, emerging from the depths of September to become an October hero, and John Wetteland to break the Braves' hearts by getting three final outs in the bottom of the tenth.

They were so destroyed by the loss that Cox would call a team meeting the next afternoon because "we were acting like we lost the World Series last night." Cox said he wanted to remind the Braves they were still on their way toward winning the Series, not losing it. But after game four it couldn't have been easy to convince them.

Game Five . . . October 24 . . . Yankees 1, Braves 0

By the time the lights went out in Georgia, only nine innings stood between the Yankees and destiny. Just nine, and the Yankees were ready to prove to the Braves that nothing was impossible. Nothing. Not in 1996, the year of living miraculously.

"People said we were done, finished, that we were coming down here to get swept," said Derek Jeter. "The more we heard that, the more we thought, 'Man, they're wrong.' And look at us—we're still alive, aren't we?"

Alive? The Yankees were on the doorstep of their first World Championship since 1978, following a heart-stopping 1–0 win in game five. Andy Pettitte and John Wetteland outpitched John Smoltz and Mark Wohlers—handing the Braves their third straight loss at Fulton County Stadium while running the Yankees' road record in October to a remarkable 8-0.

It wasn't over, not with Greg Maddux and Tom Glavine on deck. But the Yankees would have the luxury, if necessary, of two nights in a sold-out Yankee Stadium and all of New York City waiting to see the Machine of the nineties dismantled. Cecil Fielder, who launched the game-winning double in the fourth inning off Smoltz, said, "We're going home, man. The Bronx Zoo is going to be a zoo."

Over and over, the Yankees talked about the way Pettitte took the Braves apart, silencing a team that had ambushed him for seven runs in just two innings in game one. Pettitte had learned from that loss, changing speeds more this time and not challenging the Braves inside so much.

But as brilliant as Pettitte was, still another Yankee win came down to the Yankee bull pen and a sweaty ninth inning.

Torre had allowed Pettitte to start the ninth. But he gave up a leadoff double to Chipper Jones, and after Jones took third on Fred McGriff's slow roller to first base, John Wetteland arrived with just one mission: either strike out or get a ground ball from Javy Lopez.

"Just getting an out wouldn't do at that point. I knew I had to do better than that," Wetteland said.

That's why he threw Lopez a slider—late-breaking and mean, getting the ground ball he so desperately needed to keep Jones from scoring, hit right at Charlie Hayes.

With two outs Joe Torre made the bold decision to intentionally walk Ryan Klesko—willfully putting the winning run on base—so Wetteland could go one-on-one with pinch hitter Luis Polonia.

The war lasted seven pitches. Seven fastballs. Polonia fouled off the first six. The temptation was great for Leyritz to call for a slider, but lodged in his memory bank was Wohlers hanging a breaking pitch in game four, the one Leyritz himself crushed for a three-run home run.

"I told John, 'If you're going to get beat, get beat with your best. Remember what happened to Wohlers,' " Leyritz said. "It was going to be fastballs all the way."

On the seventh fastball, Polonia connected. And the race was on: his line drive to right-center against Paul O'Neill, who had been hampered throughout the postseason by a pulled left hamstring. As the ball began to carry, O'Neill seemed to be losing ground.

"My heart started pounding like crazy," O'Neill would say, "because it was really taking off on me."

He finally reached Polonia's blast at the warning track—on a full sprint, and with full extension of his glove. The Yankees instantly mobbed Wetteland on the mound, and they buried O'Neill is a sea of high-fives when he finally returned from the deepest reaches of Fulton County Stadium.

The Yankees knew they were lucky to beat Smoltz. Their only run had been unearned, thanks to miscommunication in right-center between Marquis Grissom and Jermaine Dye on Charlie Hayes's fly ball in the fourth inning.

Dye gave way to Grissom, but he had to cut in front of him to avoid a collision, and Grissom reached late for the ball, only to have it glance off his glove. The error allowed Hayes to reach second, and Cecil Fielder made the Braves pay for it, drilling a double off the wall in left—his second of three hits against Smoltz.

The run had stood up, but only because Pettitte had made a gutsy play in the sixth inning. Smoltz and Grissom had led off with back-to-back singles, and Mark Lemke bunted back toward Pettitte. The left-hander would say he'd already made up his mind to go to third on anything bunted right at him, but as he scrambled off the mound he knew it would be close.

With Leyritz shouting, "Third! Third!" Pettitte bare-handed the ball and fired to third base, just nipping Smoltz.

"That's why he won twenty-one games this season," Leyritz said of Pettitte's bare-handed play. "He's got nerve."

One pitch later, Chipper Jones lined a one-bouncer directly at Pettitte. And here is the mathematical equation for shock: 1–4–3. A Pettitte-to-Duncan-to-Fielder double play.

The inning was over. Soon the game would be, as well. The Yankees had swept through Atlanta the same way they had Cleveland and Baltimore this season. They were 18-0 in those cities, and if that wasn't a sign of destiny, the events of the next several hours had to be.

Game Six . . . October 26 . . . Yankees 3, Braves 2

By the time the Yankees landed at Newark Airport at about 3 A.M. on October 25, the last miracle of the season was in the works: Frank Torre was getting a new heart.

A twenty-eight-year-old man from the Bronx had died of a brain injury and Torre was highest on the list of eligible recipients whose blood type matched that of the donor. By 8 A.M. Joe's brother was being wheeled into the operating room for a heart transplant. The timing of the surgery, like so much of the Yankee season, was perfect, falling on the only off day of the entire Series.

Joe had gotten a phone call at 5:30 A.M., about a half-hour after arriving at his home in New Rochelle, New York. When the Yankee manager arrived at the hospital during the surgery, a doctor told him: "Frank told me to tell you: 'Good luck.' "

News spread of Torre's surgery, and people throughout the city waited anxiously for word. All of New York seemed to think of the Torres as family by now, so compelling was the saga of Joe and his brother.

Four hours after the surgery began, doctors pronounced it a success. They said Frank should even be up to watching game six on TV from the intensive care unit the next night.

Was there any doubt at this point? As Joe would say afterward, "I don't know if it was fair to the Braves. Everyone was praying for me because they felt sorry I hadn't been to the World Series in thirty years of baseball. And because of Frank."

But in game six the Yankees made Joe sweat right to the end, while providing an immediate test for Frank's new heart.

They had taken advantage of a rare lapse by Greg Maddux, ripping off a rapid-fire rally in the third inning that produced a 3–0 lead.

"He made a few mistakes and we took advantage," said Bernie Williams. Paul O'Neill hit a hanging change-up into the right-field corner for a double; Joe Girardi crushed a belt-high fastball to dead center for a triple; Derek Jeter, on a 2-and-0 cut-fastball that didn't bite, lined a single over shortstop; and

Bernie Williams muscled an inside fastball into center for still another RBI single.

Yankee Stadium was rocking with wall-to-wall noise, but the Braves came right back against Jimmy Key. They cut the lead to 3–1, and had a chance to do more when they loaded the bases with one out, but Terry Pendleton swung at a below-the-knees 3-and-1 sinker, grounding to Jeter, who started an inning-ending double play.

"Terry's an aggressive hitter," said Key. "I tried to take advantage of that."

Maddux wasn't giving away any more runs, so in the end it was up to the bull pen, the Yankees' greatest weapon, to secure one last victory. Typical of the postseason, it was a team effort: David Weathers came on with a runner on third and one out in the sixth and struck out Javy Lopez with a nasty slider. He walked Andruw Jones, but Graeme Lloyd then got pinch hitter Ryan Klesko to pop out.

"All we wanted to do," said Weathers, "was get the game to Mariano."

One more time, Mariano Rivera played Superman. He blew away the Braves in the seventh and the eighth, getting six straight outs after walking the first hitter he faced.

So finally it came down to John Wetteland. Sensational as he was in '96, Wetteland never seemed to take the easy route to a save, and, sure enough, he took the Yankees on one last roller-coaster ride. A strikeout. Two singles. A strikeout of Luis Polonia in a rematch of their game five duel produced a deafening roar, as the crowd geared up for the final out. But then a single by Marquis Grissom cut the lead to 3–2 and brought silence.

Up came Mark Lemke, such a pesky hitter that Paul O'Neill said, "He was the last guy I wanted to see up there."

With his quick, compact swing, he was tough to overmatch. But Wetteland, "so amped up that I didn't know where the ball was going," was throwing bullets. Lemke swung through one. He fouled off another that Charlie Hayes missed catching by inches, leaning into the Braves' dugout.

The suspense was unbearable in the Yankee dugout. Finally, Don Zimmer, Torre's bench coach and season-long confidant, grabbed the manager's arm and said, "This one's for Frank."

Wetteland fired one more time and Lemke was late again, popping it up toward the third-base dugout once more. But this time it stayed within reach, settling into Hayes's glove for the final out. The stadium exploded with noise while the Yankees rushed to pile on Wetteland at the mound.

Torre stayed in the dugout, hugging each of his coaches. He wasn't as emotional as he had been at the end of the Orioles series. Just joyful. He hugged his players, took them on a victory lap around Yankee Stadium as a salute to the fans, then popped the champagne one more time in the clubhouse.

"I've never been so happy," he said. "I never thought this would happen to me."

The Yankees' first World Championship since 1978 belonged to more than Torre. Bob Watson managed a smile for the first time in months, it seemed, and talked of how proud he was to represent his race as general manager of a championship team, fifty years after Jackie Robinson had broken the color line in the sport. But would he be back in 1997? He still said he couldn't answer that question.

Finally, George Steinbrenner made himself visible during a celebration for the first time in the postseason. The Boss was a winner again, the championship providing justification for the seeming chaos he'd created by breaking up a winning ball club in the off season.

But Steinbrenner wasn't gloating. He was teary-eyed himself, lauding Joe Torre and his players for their efforts, pointing out all the "wonderful human stories" that made up the 1996 Yankees.

"This is a team New York can be proud of," Steinbrenner said.

Ultimately it was his team, but it will be remembered mostly as Torre's year. He became a beloved figure, in his own clubhouse and far beyond. He had received a heartwarming ovation in Atlanta during introductions before game three, and as the first native New Yorker to manage the Yankees to a championship, he was practically regarded as family throughout the Big Apple.

Steinbrenner had proven that fans are loyal to the uniforms, not the men who wear them, but Torre's season of triumph and tragedy had touched people in a more personal way. There wasn't a Yankee fan in the five boroughs who didn't know that Torre's debt finally had been repaid.

He would keep one World Series ring for himself.

He would give another to the son of his brother Frank.

1996 Regular Season Yankee Stats

PLAYER	AVG	G	AB	R	H	2B	3B	HR	RBI	SB	CS	E
# Aldrete, M.	.213	63	108	16	23	6	0	6	20	0	1	1
NYY	.250	32	68	11	17	5	0	3	12	0	1	0
Boggs, W.	.311	132	501	80	156	29	2	2	41	1	2	7
+ De Posada, J.	.071	8	14	1	1	0	0	0	1	0	0	0
Duncan, M.	.340	109	400	62	136	34	3	8	56	4	3	12
# Eenhoorm, R.	.172	18	29	3	5	0	0	0	2	0	0	2
NYY	.071	12	14	2	1	0	0	0	2	0	0	0
# Fielder, C.	.252	160	591	85	149	20	0	39	117	0	0	7
NYY	.260	53	200	30	52	8	0	13	37	0	0	0
+ Fox, A.	.196	113	189	26	37	4	3	3	13	11	3	12
Girardi, J.	.294	124	422	55	124	22	3	2	45	13	4	3
Hayes, C.	.284	20	67	7	19	3	0	2	13	0	0	0
+ Howard, M.	.204	35	54	9	11	1	0	1	9	0	0	1
James, D.	.167	6	12	1	2	0	0	0	0	1	0	0
+ Jeter, D.	.314	157	582	104	183	25	6	10	78	14	7	22
Kelly, P.	.143	13	21	4	3	0	0	0	2	0	1	1
Leyritz, J.	.264	88	265	23	70	10	0	7	40	2	0	6
+ Luke, M.	.000	1	0	1	0	0	0	0	0	0	0	0
Martinez, T.	.292	155	595	82	174	28	0	25	117	2	1	5
McIntosh, T.	.000	3	3	0	0	0	0	0	0	0	0	0
O'Neill, P.	.302	150	546	89	165	35	1	19	91	0	1	0
Raines, T.	.284	59	201	45	57	10	0	9	33	10	0	1
+ Rivera, R.	.284	46	88	17	25	6	1	2	16	6	1	0
# Sierra, R.	.247	142	518	61	128	26	2	12	72	4	2	6
NYY	.258	96	360	39	93	17	1	11	52	1	4	6
# Sojo, L.	.220	95	287	23	63	10	1	1	21	2	3	1
NYY	.275	18	40	3	11	2	0	0	5	0	2	8
Strawberry, D.	.262	63	202	35	53	13	0	11	36	6	5	0

+ = rookie
# = combined stats for all teams played on in 1996

Batting

PLAYER	AVG	G	AB	R	H	2B	3B	HR	RBI	SB	CS	E
Williams, B.	.305	143	551	108	168	26	7	29	102	17	4	5
#Williams, G.	.252	125	325	43	82	19	4	5	34	10	9	4
NYY	.270	99	233	37	63	15	4	5	30	7	8	3
NEW YORK	.288	162	5628	871	1621	293	28	162	830	96	46	91
DH	.272	162	629	97	171	38	1	27	103	6	5	0

Pitching

PITCHER	IP	W	L	ERA	G	GS	CG	SHO	SV	H	R	ER	HR	BB	SO
Aldrete, M	1.0	0	0	0.00	1	0	0	0	0	1	0	0	0	0	0
+Boehringer, B.	46.1	2	4	5.44	15	3	0	0	0	46	28	28	6	21	37
#Bones, R.	152.0	7	14	6.22	36	24	0	0	0	184	115	105	30	68	63
NYY	7.0	0	0	14.14	4	1	0	0	0	14	11	11	2	6	8
Brewer, B.	5.2	1	0	9.53	4	0	0	0	0	7	6	6	0	8	8
Cone, D.	72.0	7	2	2.88	11	11	1	1	0	50	25	23	3	34	71
Gibson, P.	4.1	0	0	6.23	4	0	0	0	0	6	3	3	1	0	3
Gooden, D.	170.2	11	7	5.01	29	29	1	1	0	169	101	95	19	88	126
Howe, S.	17.0	0	1	6.35	25	0	0	0	0	19	12	12	1	6	5
+Hutton, M.	30.1	0	2	5.04	12	2	0	0	0	32	19	17	3	18	25
Kamieniecki, S.	22.2	1	2	11.12	7	5	0	0	0	36	30	28	6	19	15
Key, J.	169.1	12	11	4.68	30	30	0	0	0	171	93	88	21	58	116
#Lloyd, G.	56.2	2	6	4.29	65	0	0	0	0	61	30	27	4	22	30
NYY	5.2	0	2	17.47	13	0	0	0	0	12	11	11	1	5	6
+Mecir, J.	40.1	1	1	5.13	26	0	0	0	0	42	24	23	6	23	38
+Mendoza, R.	53.0	4	5	6.79	12	11	0	0	0	80	43	40	5	10	34

+ = rookie
# = combined stats for all teams played on in 1996

PITCHER	IP	W	L	ERA	G	GS	CG	SHO	SV	H	R	ER	HR	BB	SO
Nelson, J.	74.1	4	4	4.36	73	0	0	0	2	75	38	36	6	36	91
+Pavlas, D.	23.0	0	0	2.35	16	0	0	0	1	23	7	6	0	7	18
Pettitte, A.	221.0	21	8	3.87	35	34	2	0	0	229	105	95	23	72	162
Polley, E.	21.2	1	3	7.89	32	0	0	0	0	23	20	19	5	11	14
Rivera, M.	107.2	8	3	2.09	61	0	0	0	5	73	25	25	1	34	130
Rogers, K.	179.0	12	8	4.68	30	30	2	1	0	179	97	93	16	83	92
Weathers, D.	17.1	0	2	9.35	11	4	0	0	0	23	19	18	1	14	13
Wetteland, J.	63.2	2	3	2.83	62	0	0	0	43	54	23	20	9	21	69
Whitehurst, W.	8.0	1	1	6.75	2	2	0	0	0	11	6	6	1	2	1
#Wickman, B.	95.2	7	1	4.42	70	0	0	0	0	106	50	47	10	44	75
NYY	79.0	4	1	4.67	58	0	0	0	0	94	41	41	7	34	61
NEW YORK	1440.0	92	70	4.65	162	162	6	9	52	1469	787	744	143	610	1139

+ = rookie
# = combined stats for all teams played on in 1996

Division Series
New York vs. Texas

GAME 1 — 10/1/96

RANGERS 6   YANKEES 2

Texas	AB	R	H	BI	BB	SO	Avg.
Hamilton cf	4	0	0	0	0	0	.000
IRodriguez c	4	1	1	0	0	1	.250
Greer lf	3	1	1	0	1	1	.333
JGonzalez rf	4	1	1	3	0	1	.250
WClark 1b	4	1	1	0	0	0	.250
Tettleton dh	3	1	0	0	1	3	.000
Palmer 3b	4	1	2	2	0	1	.500
McLemore 2b	4	0	1	1	0	1	.250
Elster ss	4	0	1	0	0	2	.250
Totals	34	6	8	6	2	10	

New York	AB	R	H	BI	BB	SO	Avg.
Raines lf	5	1	1	0	0	1	.200
Boggs 3b	5	0	1	0	0	1	.200
O'Neill rf	4	0	0	0	0	1	.000
BeWilliams cf	4	0	1	1	0	0	.250
Martinez 1b	4	1	3	0	0	0	.750
Strawberry dh	4	0	0	0	0	2	.000
Duncan 2b	4	0	2	1	0	1	.500
Girardi c	3	0	1	0	1	0	.333
Jeter ss	4	0	1	0	0	1	.250
Totals	37	2	10	2	1	7	

Texas	000 501 000	6	8	0
New York	100 100 000	2	10	0

LOB: Texas 3, Yankees 9. 2B: Elster (1), Boggs (1), Martinez 2 (2). HR: JGonzalez (1) off Cone; Palmer (1) off Cone. RBI: JGonzalez 3 (3), Palmer 2 (2), McLemore (1), BeWilliams (1), Duncan (1). CS: McLemore (1). Runners left in scoring position: Texas 1 (Hamilton); Yankees 6 (Boggs, TiMartinez,Duncan, DJeter 3). Runners moved up: Raines, BeWilliams, Strawberry. DP: Yankees 1 (Girardi and Duncan).

Texas	IP	H	R	ER	BB	SO	NP	ERA
Burkett W, 1-0	9.0	10	2	2	1	7	122	2.00

New York	IP	H	R	ER	BB	SO	NP	ERA
Cone L, 0-1	6.0	8	6	6	2	8	118	9.00
Lloyd	1.0	0	0	0	0	0	7	0.00
Weathers	2.0	0	0	0	0	2	21	0.00

Umpires: Home, Evans; First, Kaiser; Second, Merrill; Third, Young; Left, Clark; Right, Johnson T: 2:50 A: 57,205.

GAME 2 — 10/2/96

YANKEES 5   RANGERS 4

Texas	AB	R	H	BI	BB	SO	Avg.
Hamilton cf	6	0	2	0	0	0	.200
IRodriguez c	4	0	0	0	1	2	.125
Greer lf	5	1	0	0	1	1	.125
JGonzalez rf	5	2	3	4	1	0	.444
WClark 1b	4	0	1	0	2	0	.250
Palmer 3b	6	0	1	0	0	1	.300
Tettleton dh	3	0	0	0	2	2	.000
McLemore 2b	4	0	0	0	0	2	.125
Elster ss	4	1	1	0	1	0	.250
Totals	41	4	8	4	8	8	

New York	AB	R	H	BI	BB	SO	Avg.
Raines lf	4	0	1	0	1	0	.222
Boggs 3b	3	0	0	0	1	0	.125
a-Hayes ph-3b	1	0	0	1	0	0	.000
O'Neill rf	5	0	1	0	0	0	.111
BeWilliams cf	3	1	1	0	2	0	.286
Martinez 1b	4	1	0	0	1	1	.375
Fielder dh	3	1	2	2	1	0	.667
2-Fox pr-dh	0	0	0	0	0	0	----
b-Strawberry ph-dh	1	0	0	0	0	0	.000
Duncan 2b	5	0	0	0	0	1	.222
Leyritz c	2	0	0	1	0	0	.000
1-Girardi pr-c	1	1	0	0	1	0	.250
Jeter ss	5	1	3	0	0	0	.444
Totals	37	5	8	4	6	2	

Texas	013 000 000 000	4	8	1
New York	010 100 110 001	5	8	0

No outs when winning run scored. a-hit sacrifice fly for Boggs in the 7th. b-grounded out for Fox in the 11th. 1-ran for Leyritz in the 7th. 2-ran for Fielder in the 8th. E: Palmer (1). LOB: Texas 11, Yankees 9. 2B: Elster (2), DJeter (1). HR: Fielder (1) off KHill; JGonzalez 2 (3) off Pettitte 2. RBI: JGonzalez 4 (7), Hayes (1), Fielder 2 (2), Leyritz (1). S: IRodriguez, McLemore, Raines, Hayes. SF: Hayes. GIDP: Greer. Runners left in scoring position: Texas 5 (IRodriguez, WClark, Palmer 3); Yankees 3 (O'Neill 2, Duncan). Runners moved up: IRodriguez, Greer, TiMartinez 2, Duncan, Leyritz. DP: Texas 1 (Hamilton and WClark); Yankees 1 (Pettitte, DJeter and TiMartinez)

Texas	IP	H	R	ER	BB	SO	NP	ERA
Hill	6.0	5	3	3	3	1	106	4.50
Cook H, 1	1.0	0	0	0	0	0	10	0.00
Russell BS, 1	2.1	2	1	1	0	0	25	3.86
Stanton L, 0-1	1.2	1	1	0	3	1	33	0.00
Henneman	0.0	0	0	0	0	0	1	----

New York	IP	H	R	ER	BB	SO	NP	ERA
Pettitte	6.1	4	4	4	6	3	103	5.68
MRivera	2.2	0	0	0	1	25	0.00	
Wetteland	2.0	2	0	0	1	2	32	0.00
Lloyd	0.0	1	0	0	0	0	3	0.00
Nelson	0.2	1	0	0	0	2	12	0.00
Rogers	0.0	0	0	1	0	4	----	
Boehringer W, 1-0	0.1	0	0	0	0	0	3	0.00

KHill pitched to 2 batters in the 7th, Lloyd pitched to 1 batter in the 12th, Rogers pitched to 1 batter in the 12th, Stanton pitched to 2 batters in the 12th, Henneman pitched to 1 batter in the 12th. **IBB:** off Wetteland (JGonzalez) 1. **HBP:** by KHill (Leyritz). **WP:** Pettite. **Umpires:** Home, Kaiser; First, Merrill; Second, Young; Third, Clark; Left, Johnson; Right, Evans. **T:** 4:26 **A:** 57,156.

GAME 3 — 10/4/96

YANKEES 3   RANGERS 2

New York	AB	R	H	BI	BB	SO	Avg.
Jeter ss	4	1	2	0	0	1	.462
Raines lf	3	1	1	0	1	0	.250
BeWilliams cf	3	1	2	2	0	0	.400
Fielder dh	4	0	0	0	0	1	.286
Martinez 1b	3	0	0	0	1	0	.273
Duncan 2b	3	0	2	1	0	0	.333
Sojo 2b	0	0	0	0	0	0	----
O'Neill rf	3	0	0	0	0	1	.083
RRivera ph-rf	1	0	0	0	0	1	.000
Hayes 3b	3	0	0	0	0	0	.000
Girardi c	2	0	0	0	1	0	.167
Totals	29	3	7	3	3	4	

Texas	AB	R	H	BI	BB	SO	Avg.
Hamilton cf	5	0	1	0	0	1	.200
IRodriguez c	4	0	2	1	0	0	.250
Greer lf	4	0	1	0	0	0	.167
JGonzalez rf	4	1	2	1	0	0	.462
WClark 1b	3	0	0	0	1	2	.182
Palmer 3b	4	0	0	0	0	2	.214
Tettleton dh	3	0	0	0	1	1	.000
Buford pr	0	0	0	0	0	0	----
McLemore 2b	3	0	0	0	0	1	.091
Elster ss	1	1	0	0	2	0	.222
Newson ph	1	0	0	0	0	0	.000
Totals	32	2	6	2	4	7	

New York	100	000	002	3	7	1
Texas	000	110	000	2	6	1

E: Girardi (1), Elster (1). **LOB:** Yankees 4, Texas 8. **2B:** IRodriguez (1) **HR:** JGonzalez (4) off Key; BeWilliams (1) off DOliver. **RBI:** BeWilliams 2 (3), Duncan (2), IRodriguez (1), Gonzalez (8). **SB:** Elster (1). **CS:** BeWilliams (1), Hayes (1). **S:** McLemore. **SF:** BeWilliams. **GIDP:** O'Neill 2. **Runners left in scoring position:** New York 2 (BeWilliams, RRivera), Texas 4 (Hamilton, Greer 2, Palmer). **Runners moved up:** Fielder, Girardi, JGonzalez, Newson. **DP:** Texas 2 (DOliver, Elster and WClark), (Elster, McLemore and WClark).

New York	IP	H	R	ER	BB	SO	NP	ERA
Key	5.0	5	2	2	1	3	101	3.60
Nelson W, 1-0	3.0	1	0	0	2	3	37	0.00
Wetteland S, 11.0		0	0	0	1	1	16	0.00

Texas	IP	H	R	ER	BB	SO	NP	ERA
DOliver L, 0-1	8.0	6	3	3	2	3	113	3.38
Henneman	0.2	1	0	0	1	0	3	0.00
Stanton	0.1	0	0	0	0	1	7	0.00

DOliver pitched to 2 batters in the 9th. **IBB:** off JNelson (WClark) 1, off Henneman (Martinez) 1. **HBP:** by DOliver (Duncan). **Inherited Runners Scored:** Henneman 2-2; Stanton 2-0. **Umpires:** Home, Tschida; First, Welke; Second, Shulock; Third, Hendry; Left, Coble; Right, Kosc **T:** 3:09 **A:** 50,860.

GAME 4 — 10/5/96

YANKEES 6   RANGERS 4

New York	AB	R	H	BI	BB	SO	Avg.
Raines lf	4	1	1	0	1	0	.250
Boggs 3b	4	0	0	0	0	1	.083
BeWilliams cf	5	3	3	2	0	1	.467
Martinez 1b	4	1	1	0	1	0	.267
Fielder dh	4	1	2	2	0	1	.364
1-Fox pr-dh	0	0	0	0	0	0	----
c-Leyritz ph-dh	1	0	0	0	0	1	.000
O'Neill rf	3	0	1	0	0	0	.133
a-Hayes ph	1	0	1	0	0	0	.200
RRivera rf	0	0	0	0	0	0	.000
Duncan 2b	4	0	1	1	0	2	.313
Sojo 2b	0	0	0	0	0	0	----
Girardi c	3	0	1	0	1	1	.222
Jeter ss	4	0	1	1	0	0	.412
Totals	37	6	12	6	3	7	

Texas	AB	R	H	BI	BB	SO	Avg.
Hamilton cf	4	0	0	0	0	1	.158
IRodriguez c	4	0	3	1	1	0	.375
Greer lf	4	0	0	0	1	1	.125
JGonzalez rf	3	1	1	1	2	1	.438
WClark 1b	5	0	0	0	0	1	.125
Palmer 3b	5	2	1	0	0	1	.211
Tettleton dh	3	0	1	1	1	1	.083
McLemore 2b	4	1	1	1	0	0	.133
Elster ss	3	0	2	0	0	0	.333
b-Newson ph	0	0	0	0	1	0	.000
2-Buford pr	0	0	0	0	0	0	.000
RGonzales ss	0	0	0	0	0	0	----
Totals	35	4	9	4	6	5	

New York	000	310	101	6	12	1
Texas	022	000	000	4	9	0

a-singled for O'Neill in the 7th. b-walked for Elster in the 8th. c-struck out for Fox in the 9th. 1-ran for Fielder in the 7th. 2-ran for Newson in the 8th. **E:** Jeter (1). **LOB:** Yankees 8, Texas 11. **2B:** Palmer (1). **HR:** JGonzalez (5) off Boehringer; BeWilliams 2 (3) off Pavlik, Stanton. **RBI:** BeWilliams 2 (5), Fielder 2 (4), Duncan (3), Jeter (1), IRodriguez (2), JGonzalez (9), Tettleton (1), McLemore (2). **SB:** BeWilliams (1). **S:** Boggs, Hamilton. **GIDP:** Raines, WClark. **Runners left in scoring position:** New York 4 (Boggs 2, Duncan 2); Texas 6 (Hamilton, Greer 2, WClark 2, Palmer). **Runners moved up:** Jeter. **DP:** New York 1 (Jeter, Duncan and Martinez); Texas 1 (Elster, McLemore and WClark).

New York	IP	H	R	ER	BB	SO	NP	ERA
Rogers	2.0	5	2	2	1	1	39	9.00
Boehringer	1.0	3	2	1	2	0	28	6.75
Weathers W, 1-0								
	3.0	1	0	0	0	3	42	0.00
MRivera	2.0	0	0	0	1	0	29	0.00
Wetteland S, 2								
	1.0	0	0	0	2	1	18	0.00

Texas	IP	H	R	ER	BB	SO	NP	ERA
BWitt	3.1	4	3	3	2	3	59	8.10
DPatterson	0.1	1	0	0	0	0	5	0.00
Cook	0.1	0	0	0	1	0	10	0.00
Pavlik L, 0-1	2.2	4	2	2	0	1	44	6.75
Vosberg	0.0	1	0	0	0	0	2	----
Russell	0.2	1	0	0	0	1	10	3.00
Stanton	1.1	1	1	1	0	1	18	2.70
Henneman	0.1	0	0	0	0	1	4	0.00

Boehringer pitched to 2 batters in the 4th, Vosberg pitched to 1 batter in the 7th. **WP:** BWitt **Inherited Runners Scored:** Weathers 2-0; DPatterson 2-1, Cook 2-0, Vosberg 2-0, Russell 3-0, Stanton 1-0. **Umpires:** Home, Welke; First, Shulock; Second, Hendry; Third, Coble; Left, Kosc; Right, DOliver **T:** 3:57 **A:** 50,066.

LCS
New York vs. Baltimore

GAME 1 — 10/9/96

YANKEES 5   ORIOLES 4
11 INNINGS

Baltimore	AB	R	H	BI	BB	SO	AVG
ByAnderson cf	5	1	2	1	1	1	.400
Zeile 3b	6	0	1	0	0	1	.167
RAlomar 2b	6	0	1	0	0	3	.167
RPalmeiro 1b	3	3	3	1	2	0	1.000
Bonilla rf	4	0	0	0	0	0	.000
Tarasco rf	1	0	0	0	0	1	.000
CRipken ss	5	0	2	0	0	1	.400
Murray dh	4	0	1	1	1	0	.250
Surhoff lf	3	0	0	1	0	1	.000
Devereaux lf	1	0	0	0	0	0	.000
Parent c	5	0	1	0	0	2	.200
Totals	43	4	11	4	4	10	

Yankees	AB	R	H	BI	BB	SO	AVG
Raines lf	6	1	2	0	0	0	.333
Boggs 3b	5	1	0	0	1	1	.000
BeWilliams cf	4	1	2	2	2	1	.500
TiMartinez 1b	5	0	1	0	0	1	.200
Fielder dh	2	1	0	0	3	0	.000
1-Fox pr-dh	0	0	0	0	0	0	---
O'Neill rf	3	0	0	0	0	0	.000
a-Hayes ph	0	0	0	0	0	0	---
b-Strawberry ph-rf	1	0	0	1	1	0	.000
Duncan 2b	4	0	1	0	0	1	.250
Leyritz c	4	0	1	1	0	2	.250
c-Aldrete ph	0	0	0	0	0	0	---
d-Girardi ph-c	1	0	0	0	0	0	.000
DJeter ss	5	1	4	1	0	0	.800
Totals	40	5	11	5	7	6	

Baltimore	011	101	000	00	4 11 1
Yankees	110	000	110	01	5 11 0

No outs when winning run scored. **a**-announced for O'Neill in the 7th. **b**-walked for Hayes in the 7th. **c**-announced for Leyritz in the 9th. **d**-lined into double play for Aldrete in the 9th. **1**-ran for Fielder in the 9th. **E:** RAlomar (1). **LOB:** Baltimore 11, Yankees 13. **2B:** ByAnderson (1), CRipken (1), Raines (1), BeWilliams (1). **HR:** ByAnderson (1) off Pettitte; RPalmeiro (1) off Pettitte; BeWilliams (1) off RMyers; DJeter (1) off Benitez. **RBI:** ByAnderson (1), RPalmeiro (1), Murray (1), Surhoff (1), BeWilliams 2 (2), Strawberry (1), Leyritz (1), DJeter (1). **SB:** DJeter (1). **SF:** Surhoff. **GIDP:** Raines. **Runners left in scoring position:** Baltimore 5 (RAlomar, Bonilla, Surhoff, Devereaux, Parent); Yankees 6 (Raines, TiMartinez 2, Duncan 2, DJeter). **Runners moved up:** Murray, Boggs 2, BeWilliams, Duncan, Leyritz. **DP:** Baltimore 2 (CRipken and RAlomar), (Zeile, RAlomar and RPalmeiro).

Baltimore	IP	H	R	ER	BB	SO	TP	ERA
Erickson	6.1	7	3	2	3	3	98	2.84
Orosco	.1	0	0	0	1	1	7	0.00
Benitez	1.0	2	1	1	2	2	24	9.00
ARhodes	.1	0	0	0	1	0	14	0.00
TeMathews	.1	0	0	0	1	0	11	0.00
RMyers L, 0-1								
	1.2	2	1	1	0	0	16	5.40

Yankees	IP	H	R	ER	BB	SO	TP	ERA
Pettitte	7.0	7	4	4	4	4	124	5.14
JNelson	1.0	0	0	0	1	0	10	0.00
Wetteland W, 1-0	1.0	1	0	0	0	2	18	0.00
MRivera W								
	2.0	3	0	0	0	3	44	0.00

RMyers pitched to 1 batter in the 11th. **IBB:** off Benitez (BeWilliams) 1, off Orosco (Fielder) 1. **HBP:** by TeMathews (Duncan). **Balk**-Pettite. **T:** 4:24. **A:** 56,495.

GAME 2 — 10/10/96

ORIOLES 5   YANKEES 3

Baltimore	AB	R	H	BI	BB	SO	AVG
ByAnderson cf	4	2	1	0	1	1	.333
Zeile 3b	4	1	2	2	1	0	.300
RAlomar 2b	4	1	2	1	0	0	.300
RPalmeiro 1b	4	1	1	2	1	1	.571
Bonilla rf	4	0	0	0	0	4	.000
Tarasco rf	0	0	0	0	0	0	.000
CRipken ss	5	0	2	0	0	0	.400
Murray dh	4	0	1	0	0	1	.250
Surhoff lf	4	0	1	0	0	0	.143
Deveraux lf	0	0	0	0	0	0	.000
Hoiles c	3	0	0	0	1	0	.000
Totals	36	5	10	5	5	7	

Yankees	AB	R	H	BI	BB	SO	AVG
DJeter ss	5	1	2	0	0	2	.600
Raines lf	4	1	1	0	1	1	.300
BeWilliams cf	3	0	2	1	2	1	.571
Fielder dh	5	0	1	1	0	0	.143
TiMartinez 1b	4	0	0	0	0	0	.111
Duncan 2b	4	0	1	0	0	1	.250
O'Neill rf	2	0	1	0	1	1	.200
a-Leyritz ph-rf	1	0	0	0	0	0	.200
Hayes 3b	4	0	1	0	0	2	.250
Girardi c	4	1	2	0	0	0	.400
Totals	36	3	11	2	4	8	

Baltimore	002	000	210		5	10	0	0
Yankees	200	000	100		3	11	1	

a-grounded out for O'Neill in the 8th. **E:** Duncan (1). **LOB:** Baltimore 10, Yankees 11. **2B:** RAlomar (1), Duncan (1). **3B:** Girardi (1). **HR:** Zeile (1) off Cone; RPalmeiro (2) off JNelson. **RBI:** Zeile 2 (2), RAlomar (1), RPalmeiro 2 (3), BeWilliams (3), Fielder (1). **SF:** RAlomar. **GIDP:** Fielder, Duncan. **Runners left in scoring position:** Baltimore 6 (ByAnderson 2, CRipken 2, Surhoff, Hoiles); Yankees 4 (Fielder, TiMartinez 2, Hayes.) **Runners moved up:** Surhoff. **DP:** Baltimore 2 (RAlomar, CRipken and RPalmeiro), (Zeile, RAlomar and RPalemeiro); Yankees 1 (O'Neill and TiMartinez).

Baltimore	IP	H	R	ER	BB	SO	TP	ERA
DWells W, 1-0								
	6.2	8	3	3	3	6	104	4.05
Mills	0.0	1	0	0	0	0	3	---
Orosco	1.1	0	0	0	0	1	19	0.00
RMyers	.1	1	0	0	1	1	17	4.50
Benitez S, 1	.2	0	0	0	0	0	12	5.40

Yankees	IP	H	R	ER	BB	SO	TP	ERA
Cone	6.0	5	2	2	5	5	133	3.00
JNelson L, 0-1								
	1.1	5	3	3	0	1	34	11.57
Lloyd	1.1	0	0	0	0	1	14	0.00
Weathers	.1	0	0	0	0	0	5	0.00

Mills pitched to 1 batter in the 7th. **Inherited runners-scored:** Mills 2-1, Orosco 2-0, Benitez 2-0, Lloyd 2-1. **HBP:** by DWells (TiMartinez). **WP:** Cone. **Umpires:** Home, Scott; First, Reilly; Second, Morrison; Third, Roe; Left, Garcia; Right, Barnett. **T:** 4:13. **A:** 56,432

GAME 3 — 10/11/96

YANKEES 5   ORIOLES 2

Yankees	AB	R	H	BI	BB	SO	AVG
Raines lf	5	0	1	0	0	0	.267
DJeter ss	4	1	1	0	0	1	.500
BeWilliams cf	3	2	1	1	1	1	.500
TiMartinez, 1b	4	1	2	0	0	0	.231
Fielder dh	4	1	1	3	0	2	.182
Strawberry rf	4	0	1	0	0	1	.200
Duncan 2b	4	0	0	0	0	1	.167
Sojo 2b	0	0	0	0	0	0	.000
Hayes 3b	2	0	0	0	2	0	.167
Girardi c	4	0	1	0	0	1	.333
Totals	34	5	8	4	3	7	

Baltimore	AB	R	H	BI	BB	SO	AVG
ByAnderson cf	4	1	1	0	0	2	.308
Zeile 3b	4	1	1	2	0	0	.286
RAlomar 2b	4	0	0	0	0	0	.214
RPalmeiro 1b	3	0	0	0	0	0	.400
Bonilla rf	3	0	0	0	0	0	.000
CRipken ss	3	0	0	0	0	1	.308
Murray dh	2	0	0	0	1	1	.200
Surhoff lf	3	0	1	0	0	1	.200
Hoiles c	3	0	0	0	0	1	.000
Totals	29	2	3	2	1	6	

Yankees	000	100	040		5	8	0	
Baltimore	200	000	000		2	3	2	

E: CRipken, Zeile. **LOB:** New York 5, Baltimore 1. **2B:** DJeter (1), TiMartinez (1). **HR:** Zeile (2) off Key; Fielder (1) off Mussina. **RBI:** BeWilliams (4), Fielder 3 (4), Zeile 2 (4). **GIDP:** Duncan, Girardi, Surhoff. **Runners left in scoring position:** New York 2 (DJeter 2). **Runners moved up:** Raines, Fielder. **DP:** New York 1 (TiMartinez); Baltimore 2 (CRipken, RAlomar and RPalmeiro), (CRipken, RAlomar, and RPalmeiro).

Yankees	IP	H	R	ER	BB	SO	TP	ERA
Key W, 1-0	8	3	2	2	1	5	117	2.25
Wetteland S, 1								
	1.0	0	0	0	0	1	12	0.00

Baltimore	IP	H	R	ER	BB	SO	TP	ERA
Mussina L, 0-1								
	7.2	8	5	5	2	6	108	5.87
Orosco	.1	0	0	0	0	2	0.00	
TeMathews	1	0	0	0	1	1	13	0.00

Umpires: Home, Reilly; First, Morrison; Second, Roe; Third, Garcia; Left, Barnett; Right, Scott. **T:** 2:50. **A:** 48,635

GAME 4 — 10/12/96

YANKEES 8   ORIOLES 4

Yankees	AB	R	H	BI	BB	SO	AVG
DJeter ss	5	1	1	0	0	2	.421
Boggs 3b	5	0	0	0	0	1	.000
BeWilliams cf	4	2	2	2	0	0	.500
TiMartinez 1b	4	1	1	0	0	0	.235
Fielder dh	4	0	0	1	0	1	.133
Strawberry lf	4	3	3	3	0	1	.444
Raines lf	0	0	0	0	0	0	.267
O'Neill rf	3	1	1	2	1	1	.250
Duncan 2b	3	0	1	0	0	0	.200
Sojo 2b	1	0	0	0	0	0	.000
Girardi c	3	0	0	0	1	2	.250
Totals	36	8	9	8	2	8	

Baltimore	AB	R	H	BI	BB	SO	AVG
ByAnderson cf	4	1	0	0	1	1	.235
Zeile 3b	5	0	2	0	0	0	.316
RAlomar 2b	5	0	2	0	0	1	.263
RPalmeiro 1b	3	0	0	1	1	2	.308
Bonilla rf	5	0	0	0	0	0	.000
CRipken ss	3	1	1	0	1	0	.313
Incaviglia dh	2	1	1	0	0	0	.500
b-Murray ph-dh	2	0	1	0	0	0	.250
Deveraux lf	1	0	0	0	0	1	.000
a-Surhoff ph-lf	3	0	2	1	0	0	.308
Hoiles c	4	1	2	2	0	1	.200
Totals	37	4	11	4	3	6	

a-singled for Incaviglia in the 4th. b-popped out for Murray in the 7th. **LOB:** New York 3, Baltimore 10. **2B:** DJeter (2), BeWilliams (2), Duncan (2), RAlomar (2). **HR:** Hoiles (1) off Rogers; BeWilliams (2) off Coppinger; Strawberry 2 (2) off Coppinger, Benitez; O'Neill (1) off Coppinger. **RBI:** BeWilliams 2 (6), Fielder (5), Strawberry 3 (4), O'Neill 2 (2), RPalmeiro (4), Surhoff (2), Hoiles 2 (2). **SF:** RPalmeiro. **Runners left in scoring positon:** New York 1 (DJeter); Baltimore 5 (Zeile 3, Bonilla, CRipken). **Runners moved up:** Boggs, Fielder, ByAnderson, Bonilla, Hoiles.

Yankees	IP	H	R	ER	BB	SO	TP	ERA
Rogers	3	5	4	4	2	3	72	12.0
Weathers W, 1-0	2.2	3	0	0	0	0	45	0.00
Lloyd	.1	0	0	0	0	0	3	0.00
MRivera	2	3	0	0	1	2	36	0.00
Wetteland	1	0	0	0	1	1	17	0.00

Baltimore	IP	H	R	ER	BB	SO	TP	ERA
Coppinger L, 0-1	5.1	6	5	5	1	3	87	8.44
ARhodes	.2	0	0	0	0	1	11	0.00
Mills	1.1	1	1	1	0	2	19	6.75
Orosco	0	1	1	1	0	0	6	4.50
Benitez	.2	1	1	1	1	0	15	7.71
TeMathews	1	0	0	0	0	12	9	0.00

Rogers pithced to 2 batters in the 4th, Orosco pitched to 1 batter in the 8th. **Inherited runners-scored:** Weathers 2-2, Lloyd 1-0, Orosco 1-0, Benitez 2-2. **WP:** Rogers. **Umpires:** Home, Morrison; First, Roe; Second, Garcia; Third, Barnett; Left, Scott; Right, Barnett. **T:** 3:45. **A:** 48,974

GAME 5 — 10/13/96

YANKEES 6   ORIOLES 4

Yankees	AB	R	H	BI	BB	SO	AVG
DJeter ss	5	1	2	0	0	0	.417
Boggs 3b	5	0	2	0	0	1	.133
BeWilliams cf	5	1	2	0	0	1	.474
TiMartinez 1b	5	1	0	0	0	1	.182
Fielder dh	3	1	1	3	1	2	.167
1-Fox pr-dh	0	0	0	0	0	0	---
b-Hayes ph-dh	1	0	0	0	0	0	.143
Strawberry lf	3	1	1	1	1	0	.417
Raines lf	0	0	0	0	0	0	.267
O'Neill rf	3	0	1	0	1	0	.273
Leyritz c	3	1	1	1	1	2	.250
Sojo 2b	4	0	1	0	0	1	.200
Totals	37	6	11	5	4	8	

Baltimore	AB	R	H	BI	BB	SO	AVG
ByAnderson cf	4	0	0	0	0	0	.190
Zeile 3b	3	1	2	1	1	0	.364
RAlomar 2b	4	1	0	0	0	0	.217
RPalmeiro 1b	4	0	0	0	0	1	.235
Bonilla rf	4	1	2	0	0	0	.050
CRipken ss	4	0	0	0	0	2	.250
Murray dh	3	1	1	1	0	0	.267
Surhoff lf	2	0	0	0	1	0	.267
Parent c	1	0	0	0	0	0	.167
a-Hoiles ph-c	2	0	0	0	0	1	.167
Totals	31	4	4	4	2	4	

Yankees	006	000	000		6	11	0
Baltimore	000	001	012		4	4	1

a-struck out for parent in the 7th. b-popped out for Fox in the 9th. 1-ran for Fielder in the 8th. **E:** RAlomar (2). **LOB:** Yankees 8, Baltimore 2. **2B:** BeWilliams (3). **HR:** Zeile (3) off Pettitte; Bonilla (1) off Wetteland; Murray (1) off Pettitte; Fielder (2) off Erickson; Strawberry (3) off Erickson; Leyritz (1) off Erickson. **RBI:** Fielder 3 (8), Strawberry (5), Leyritz (2), Zeile (5), Bonilla 2 (2), Murray (2). **SB:** DJeter (2), BeWilliams (1). **GIDP:** O'Neill. **Runners left in scoring position:** Yankees 5 (DJeter 2, Boggs, TiMartinez 2). **Runners moved up:** TiMartinez, Strawberry. **DP:** Baltimore 1 (CRipken, RAlomar and RPalmeiro).

Yankees	IP	H	R	ER	BB	SO	TP	ERA
Pettitte W, 1-0	8	3	2	2	1	3	100	3.60
Wetteland	1	1	2	2	1	1	20	4.50

Baltimore	IP	H	R	ER	BB	SO	TP	ERA
Erickson L, 0-1	5	7	6	1	1	5	92	2.38
ARhodes	1	2	0	0	0	1	19	0.00
Mills	1	1	0	0	1	1	17	3.86
RMyers	2	1	0	0	2	1	38	2.25

Mills pitched to 1 batter in the 8th. **Runners inherited-scored:** RMyers 1-0. **WP:** ARhodes. **Umpires:** Home, Roe; First, Garcia; Second, Barnett; Third, Scott; Left, Reilly; Right, Morrison. **T:** 2:57. **A:** 48,718

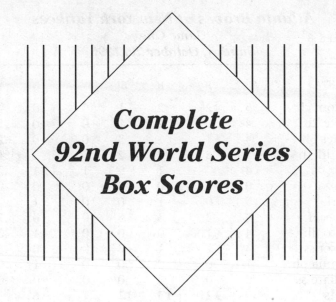

*Complete
92nd World Series
Box Scores*

Atlanta Braves at New York Yankees
Game One
Sunday, October 20, 1996

ATLANTA	AB	R	H	BI	W	K	AVG.
Grissom cf	5	2	2	1	0	0	.400
Lemke 2b	4	0	2	1	0	0	.500
CJones 3b	4	1	1	3	0	0	.250
McGriff 1b	5	2	2	2	0	2	.400
Lopez c	4	2	1	0	1	1	.250
Perez c	0	0	0	0	0	0	.000
Dye rf	5	0	1	0	0	1	.200
AJones lf	4	3	3	5	0	0	.750
Klesko dh	4	1	0	0	0	1	.000
Blauser ss	3	1	1	0	0	0	.333
Polonia ph	1	0	0	0	0	1	.000
Belliard ss	0	0	0	0	0	0	.000
Totals	**39**	**12**	**13**	**12**	**1**	**6**	

NEW YORK	AB	R	H	BI	W	K	AVG.
Jeter ss	3	1	0	0	1	1	.000
Boggs 3b	4	0	2	1	0	0	.500
Williams cf	3	0	0	0	1	1	.000
Martinez 1b	3	0	1	0	1	1	.333
Fielder dh	4	0	0	0	0	1	.000
Strawberry lf	3	0	0	0	0	0	.000
Raines lf	1	0	0	0	0	0	.000
O'Neill rf	2	0	0	0	1	0	.000
Aldrete rf	0	0	0	0	0	0	.000
Hayes ph	1	0	0	0	0	0	.000
Duncan 2b	3	0	0	0	0	0	.000
Fox 2b	0	0	0	0	0	0	.000
Sojo ph	1	0	0	0	0	0	.000
Leyritz c	3	0	1	0	1	1	.333
Totals	**31**	**1**	**4**	**1**	**5**	**5**	

```
Atlanta      0 2 6  0 1 3  0 0 0 — 12
New York     0 0 0  0 1 0  0 0 0 —  1
```

E: Duncan. **LOB:** Atlanta 3, New York 8. **2B:** Boggs. **HR:** Jones (1) off Pettitte, AJones (2) off Boehringer, McGriff (1) off Boehringer. **SB:** CJones (1). **S:** Lemke. **SF:** CJones.

ATLANTA	IP	H	R	ER	BB	SO	HR	ERA
Smoltz (W 1-0)	6	2	1	1	5	4	0	1.50
McMichael	1	2	0	0	0	1	0	0.00
Neagle	1	0	0	0	0	0	0	0.00
Wade	⅔	0	0	0	0	0	0	0.00
Clontz	⅓	0	0	0	0	0	0	0.00

NEW YORK	IP	H	R	ER	BB	SO	HR	ERA
Pettitte (L 0-1)	2⅓	6	7	7	1	1	1	27.00
Boehringer	3	5	5	4	0	2	2	12.00
Weathers	1⅔	1	0	0	0	0	0	0.00
Nelson	1	1	0	0	0	1	0	0.00
Wetteland	1	0	0	0	0	2	0	0.00

T: 3:02. **A:** 56,365.
Umpires: Home, Evans (AL); First, Tata (NL); Second, Welke (AL); Third, Rippley (NL); Left, Young (AL); Right, Davis (NL).

Atlanta Braves at New York Yankees
Game Two
Monday, October 21, 1996

ATLANTA	AB	R	H	BI	W	K	AVG.
Grissom cf	5	1	2	1	0	1	.400
Lemke 2b	4	2	2	0	0	0	.500
CJones 3b	3	0	1	0	1	1	.286
McGriff 1b	3	0	2	3	0	1	.500
Lopez c	4	0	1	0	0	0	.250
Dye rf	4	0	1	0	0	0	.222
AJones lf	3	0	0	0	0	1	.429
Pendleton dh	4	1	1	0	0	1	.250
Blauser ss	2	0	0	0	1	0	.200
Polonia ph	1	0	0	0	0	0	.000
Belliard ss	0	0	0	0	0	0	.000
Totals	**33**	**4**	**10**	**4**	**2**	**5**	

NEW YORK	AB	R	H	BI	W	K	AVG.
Raines lf	4	0	2	0	0	0	.400
Boggs 3b	4	0	1	0	0	0	.375
Williams cf	4	0	0	0	0	1	.000
Martinez 1b	4	0	0	0	0	2	.143
Fielder dh	4	0	2	0	0	0	.250
Fox pr-dh	0	0	0	0	0	0	.000
O'Neill rf	4	0	1	0	0	1	.167
Duncan 2b	3	0	0	0	0	1	.000
Girardi c	3	0	0	0	0	0	.000
Jeter ss	2	0	1	0	0	0	.200
Totals	**32**	**0**	**7**	**0**	**0**	**5**	

```
Atlanta      1 0 1   0 1 1   0 0 0 — 4
New York     0 0 0   0 0 0   0 0 0 — 0
```

E: Raines. **LOB:** Atlanta 7, New York 6. **2B:** Grissom, Lemke, CJones, Pendleton, O'Neill. **CS:** Raines. **S:** Lemke. **SF:** McGriff. **GIDP:** Lopez, Blauser, Boggs. **DP:** Atlanta 1 (Lemke,

Blauser and McGriff); New York 2 (Duncan, Jeter and Martinez), (Key, Duncan and Martinez).

ATLANTA	IP	H	R	ER	BB	SO	HR	ERA
Maddux (W 1-0)	8	6	0	0	0	2	0	0.00
Wohlers	1	1	0	0	0	3	0	0.00

NEW YORK	IP	H	R	ER	BB	SO	HR	ERA
Key (L 0-1)	6	10	4	4	2	0	0	6.00
Lloyd	⅔	0	0	0	0	2	0	0.00
Nelson	1⅓	0	0	0	0	2	0	0.00
MRivera	1	0	0	0	0	1	0	0.00

HBP: by Key (AJones), by Maddux (Jeter).
T: 2:44. **A:** 56,340.
Umpires: Home, Tata (NL); First, Welke (AL); Second, Rippley (NL); Third, Young (AL); Left, Davis (NL); Right, Evans (AL).

New York Yankees at Atlanta Braves
Game Three
Tuesday, October 22, 1996

NEW YORK	AB	R	H	BI	W	K	AVG.
Raines lf	4	1	1	0	1	0	.333
Jeter ss	3	1	1	0	1	1	.250
Williams cf	5	2	2	3	0	1	.167
Fielder 1b	3	0	1	0	1	0	.273
Fox pr	0	1	0	0	0	0	---
Martinez 1b	0	0	0	0	1	0	.143
Hayes 3b	5	0	0	0	0	3	.000
Strawberry rf	3	0	1	1	1	2	.167
Duncan 2b	3	0	1	0	0	1	.111
Sojo 2b	1	0	1	1	0	0	.500
Girardi c	2	0	0	0	1	2	.000
Cone p	2	0	0	0	0	1	.000
Leyritz ph	1	0	0	0	0	0	.250
MRivera p	1	0	0	0	0	0	.000
Lloyd p	0	0	0	0	0	0	---
Wetteland p	0	0	0	0	0	0	---
Totals	**33**	**5**	**8**	**5**	**6**	**11**	

ATLANTA	AB	R	H	BI	W	K	AVG.
Grissom cf	4	1	3	0	0	0	.500
Lemke 2b	4	0	1	1	0	0	.417
CJones 3b	3	0	1	0	1	1	.300
McGriff 1b	3	0	0	0	1	0	.364
Klesko lf	3	0	0	1	1	2	.000
Lopez c	4	0	1	0	0	0	.250
AJones rf	4	0	0	0	0	2	.273
Blauser ss	4	0	0	0	0	2	.111
Glavine p	1	1	0	0	1	0	.000
Polonia ph	0	0	0	0	1	0	.000
McMichael p	0	0	0	0	0	0	---
Clontz p	0	0	0	0	0	0	---
Bielecki p	0	0	0	0	0	0	---

	AB	R	H	BI	W	K	AVG.
Pendleton ph	1	0	0	0	0	0	.200
Totals	**31**	**2**	**6**	**2**	**5**	**7**	

```
New York   1 0 0  1 0 0  0 3 0 — 5
Atlanta    0 0 0  0 0 1  0 1 0 — 2
```

E: Blauser, Jeter. **LOB:** New York 9, Atlanta 7. **2B:** Fielder. **3B:** Grissom. **HR:** Williams (1) off McMichael. **CS:** AJones, Polonia. **S:** Jeter, Girardi. **GIDP:** Lemke. **DP:** New York 1 (Fielder, Jeter and Fielder); Atlanta 1 (AJones and McGriff).

NEW YORK	IP	H	R	ER	BB	SO	HR	ERA
Cone (W 1-0)	6	4	1	1	4	3	0	1.50
MRivera	1 ⅓	2	1	1	1	1	0	3.86
Lloyd	⅔	0	0	0	0	1	0	0.00
Wetteland (S 1)	1	0	0	0	0	2	0	0.00

ATLANTA	IP	H	R	ER	BB	SO	HR	ERA
Glavine (L 0-1)	7	4	2	1	3	8	0	1.29
McMichael	0	3	3	3	0	0	1	27.00
Clontz	1	1	0	0	1	1	0	0.00
Bielecki	1	0	0	0	2	2	0	0.00

McMichael pitched to 3 batters in the 8th.

IBB: off Clontz (Strawberry).
T: 3:22. **A:** 51,843.
Umpires: Home, Welke (AL); First, Rippley (NL); Second, Young (AL); Third, Davis (NL); Left, Evans (AL); Right, Tata (NL).

New York Yankees at Atlanta Braves
Game Four
Wednesday, October 23, 1996

NEW YORK	AB	R	H	BI	W	K	AVG.
Raines lf	5	1	0	0	1	1	.214
Jeter ss	4	2	2	0	2	2	.333
Williams cf	4	1	0	0	2	1	.125
Fielder 1b	4	1	2	1	1	0	.333
Fox pr-3b	0	0	0	0	0	0	.000
Boggs ph-3b	0	0	0	1	1	0	.375
Hayes 3b-1b	5	1	3	1	1	0	.273
Strawberry rf	5	0	2	0	1	2	.273
Duncan 2b	5	1	0	0	0	1	.071
Girardi c	2	0	0	0	0	0	.000
O'Neill ph	1	0	0	0	0	1	.143
Leyritz c	2	1	1	3	0	0	.333
Rogers p	1	0	1	0	0	0	1.000
Boehringer p	0	0	0	0	0	0	.000
Sojo ph	1	0	1	0	0	0	.667
Weathers p	0	0	0	0	0	0	.000
Martinez ph	1	0	0	0	0	1	.125
Nelson p	0	0	0	0	0	0	.000
Aldrete ph	1	0	0	0	0	0	.000
MRivera p	0	0	0	0	0	0	.000
Lloyd p	1	0	0	0	0	0	.000
Wetteland p	0	0	0	0	0	0	.000
Totals	**42**	**8**	**12**	**6**	**9**	**9**	

ATLANTA	AB	R	H	BI	W	K	AVG.
Grissom cf	5	0	1	2	0	0	.421
Lemke 2b	5	0	1	0	0	1	.353
CJones 3b-ss	3	2	1	0	2	0	.308
McGriff 1b	3	1	2	1	2	0	.429
Clontz p	0	0	0	0	0	0	.000
Lopez c	2	1	0	1	1	1	.214
Wohlers p	0	0	0	0	0	0	.000

	AB	R	H	BI	W	K	AVG.
Avery p	0	0	0	0	0	0	.000
Klesko 1b	1	0	0	0	0	1	.000
AJones lf	4	1	3	1	1	1	.400
Dye rf	4	0	0	0	0	0	.154
Blauser ss	3	1	1	1	0	2	.167
Belliard ss	0	0	0	0	0	0	.000
Polonia ph	1	0	0	0	0	1	.000
Pendleton 3b	1	0	0	0	0	0	.167
Neagle p	1	0	0	0	0	1	.000
Wade p	0	0	0	0	0	0	.000
Bielecki p	1	0	0	0	0	1	.000
Perez c	1	0	0	0	0	0	.000
Totals	**35**	**6**	**9**	**6**	**6**	**9**	

```
New York   0 0 0   0 0 3   0 3 0   2 — 8
Atlanta    0 4 1   0 1 0   0 0 0   0 — 6
```

E: Dye, Klesko. **LOB:** New York 13, Atlanta 8. **2B:** Grissom, AJones. **HR:** Leyritz (1), off Wohlers, McGriff (2) off Rogers. **S:** Neagle, Dye. **SF:** Lopez. **GIDP:** Williams, McGriff. **DP:** New York 1 (Jeter, Duncan and Hayes); Atlanta 1 (Blauser, Lemke and McGriff).

NEW YORK	IP	H	R	ER	BB	SO	HR	ERA
Rogers	2	5	5	5	2	0	1	22.50
Boehringer	2	0	0	0	0	3	0	5.40
Weathers	1	1	1	1	2	2	0	3.37
Nelson	2	0	0	0	1	2	0	0.00
MRivera	1⅓	2	0	0	1	1	0	2.45
Lloyd (W 1-0)	1	0	0	0	0	1	0	0.00
Wetteland (S 2)	⅔	1	0	0	0	0	0	0.00

ATLANTA	IP	H	R	ER	BB	SO	HR	ERA
Neagle	5	5	3	2	4	3	0	3.00
Wade	0	0	0	0	1	0	0	0.00

	IP	H	R	ER	BB	SO	HR	ERA
Bielecki	2	0	0	0	1	4	0	0.00
Wohlers	2	6	3	3	0	1	1	9.00
Avery (L 0-1)	⅔	1	2	1	3	0	0	13.50
Clontz	⅓	0	0	0	0	1	0	0.00

Rogers pitched to 2 batters in the 3rd.
Neagle pitched to 4 batters in the 6th.
Wade pitched to 1 batter in the 6th.

IBB: off Weathers (McGriff); off Avery (Williams).
BK: Weathers.
T: 4:19. **A:** 51,881.
Umpires: Home, Rippley (NL); First, Young (AL); Second, Davis (NL); Third, Evans (AL); Left, Tata (NL); Right, Welke (AL).

New York Yankees at Atlanta Braves
Game Five
Thursday, October 24, 1996

NEW YORK	AB	R	H	BI	W	K	AVG.
Jeter ss	4	0	0	0	0	1	.250
Hayes 3b	4	1	0	0	0	2	.200
Williams cf	4	0	0	0	0	2	.100
Fielder 1b	4	0	3	1	0	1	.421
Martinez 1b	0	0	0	0	0	0	.125
Strawberry lf	3	0	0	0	1	1	.214
O'Neill rf	2	0	0	0	2	0	.111
Duncan 2b	4	0	0	0	0	1	.056
Sojo 2b	0	0	0	0	0	0	.667
Leyritz c	2	0	1	0	2	1	.375
Pettitte p	4	0	0	0	0	1	.375
Wetteland p	0	0	0	0	0	0	.000
Totals	**31**	**1**	**4**	**1**	**5**	**10**	

ATLANTA	AB	R	H	BI	W	K	AVG.
Grissom cf	3	0	2	0	1	1	.455
Lemke 2b	4	0	0	0	0	2	.286
CJones 3b	4	0	1	0	0	0	.294
McGriff 1b	3	0	0	0	1	1	.353
Lopez c	4	0	0	0	0	0	.167
AJones lf	2	0	1	0	1	0	.412
Klesko ph	0	0	0	0	1	0	.000
Dye rf	3	0	0	0	0	0	.125
Polonia ph	1	0	0	0	0	0	.000
Blauser ss	3	0	0	0	0	0	.133
Smoltz p	2	0	1	0	0	0	.136
Mordecai ph	1	0	0	0	0	0	.000
Wohlers p	0	0	0	0	0	0	.000
Totals	**30**	**0**	**5**	**0**	**4**	**4**	

```
New York   0 0 0   1 0 0   0 0 0 — 1
Atlanta    0 0 0   0 0 0   0 0 0 — 0
```

E: Jeter, Grissom. **LOB:** New York 8, Atlanta 7. **2B:** Fielder, CJones. **SB:** Leyritz (1), Duncan (1), AJones (1), Grissom (1). **CS:** AJones. **GIDP:** Lopez, CJones. **DP:** New York 2 (Duncan, Jeter and Fielder), (Pettitte, Duncan and Fielder); Atlanta 1 (McGriff).

NEW YORK	IP	H	R	ER	BB	SO	HR	ERA
Pettitte (W 1-1)	8 ⅓	5	0	0	3	4	0	5.91
Wetteland (S 3)	⅔	0	0	0	1	0	0	0.00

ATLANTA	IP	H	R	ER	BB	SO	HR	ERA
Smoltz (L 1-1)	8	4	1	0	3	10	0	0.64
Wohlers	1	0	0	0	2	0	0	6.75

WP: Wohlers.
IBB: off Wohlers (Leyritz), off Wetteland (Klesko).
T: 2:54. **A:** 51,881.
Umpires: Home, Young (AL); First, Davis (NL); Second, Evans (AL); Third, Tata (NL); Left, Welke (AL); Right, Rippley (NL).

Atlanta Braves at New York Yankees
Game Six
Saturday, October 25, 1996

ATLANTA	AB	R	H	BI	W	K	AVG.
Grissom cf	5	0	2	1	0	0	.444
Lemke 2b	5	0	0	0	0	0	.231
CJones 3b	4	0	1	0	0	0	.286
McGriff 1b	3	1	0	0	1	0	.300
Lopez c	3	0	1	0	1	2	.190
AJones lf-rf	3	0	1	0	1	2	.400
Dye rf	1	0	0	1	1	0	.118
Klesko ph-lf	2	1	1	0	0	0	.100
Pendleton dh	3	0	1	0	1	0	.222
Belliard pr-dh	0	0	0	0	0	0	.000
Blauser ss	3	0	1	0	0	0	.167
Polonia ph	1	0	0	0	0	1	.000
Totals	**33**	**2**	**8**	**2**	**5**	**5**	

NEW YORK	AB	R	H	BI	W	K	AVG.
Jeter ss	4	1	1	1	0	1	.250
Boggs 3b	3	0	0	0	0	0	.273
Hayes 3b	1	0	0	0	0	0	.188
Williams cf	4	0	2	1	0	0	.167
Fielder dh	4	0	1	0	0	0	.391
Martinez 1b	3	0	0	0	0	1	.091
Strawberry lf	2	0	0	0	1	1	.188
O'Neill rf	3	1	1	0	0	0	.167
Duncan 2b	1	0	0	0	0	0	.053
Sojo 2b	2	0	1	0	0	0	.600
Girardi c	3	1	2	1	0	0	.200
Totals	**30**	**3**	**8**	**3**	**1**	**3**	

Atlanta	0 0 0	1 0 0	0 0 1 — 2				
New York	0 0 3	0 0 0	0 0 x — 3				

E: Duncan. **LOB:** Atlanta 9, New York 4. **2B:** Blauser, O'Neill, CJones, Sojo. **3B:** Girardi. **SB:** Jeter (1), Williams (1). **CS:** Pendleton. **GIDP:** Pendleton, Jeter, O'Neill. **DP:** Atlanta 2 (CJones, Lemke and McGriff), (McGriff and Lemke). New York 1 (Jeter and Martinez).

ATLANTA	IP	H	R	ER	BB	SO	HR	ERA
Maddux (L 1-1)	7⅔	8	3	3	1	3	0	1.72
Wohlers	⅓	0	0	0	0	0	0	6.23

NEW YORK	IP	H	R	ER	BB	SO	HR	ERA
Key (W 1-1)	5⅓	5	1	1	3	1	0	3.97
Weathers	⅓	0	0	0	1	1	0	3.00
Lloyd	⅓	0	0	0	0	0	0	0.00
Rivera	2	0	0	0	1	1	0	1.59
Wetteland (S 4)	1	3	1	1	0	2	0	2.08

T: 2:52. **A:** 56,375.
Umpires: Home, Davis (NL); First, Evans (AL); Second, Tata (NL); Third, Welke (AL); Left, Rippley (NL); Right, Young (AL).

World Series
Composite Box Score
Atlanta vs. New York

ATLANTA	G	AVG.	AB	R	H	2B	3B	HR	RBI	BB	SO	SB	CS	E
Smoltz p	2	.500	2	0	1	0	0	0	0	0	0	0	0	0
M.Grissom cf	6	.444	27	4	12	2	1	0	5	1	2	1	0	1
A.Jones lf-rf	6	.400	20	4	8	1	0	2	6	3	6	1	2	0
F.McGriff 1b	6	.300	20	4	6	0	0	2	6	5	4	0	0	0
C.Jones 3b-ss	6	.286	21	3	6	3	0	0	3	4	2	1	0	0
M.Lemke 2b	6	.231	26	2	6	1	0	0	2	0	3	0	0	0
T.Pendleton dh-3b	4	.222	9	1	2	1	0	0	0	1	1	0	1	0
J.Lopez c	6	.190	21	3	4	0	0	0	1	3	4	0	0	0
J.Blauser ss	6	.167	18	2	3	1	0	0	1	1	4	0	0	1
J.Dye rf	5	.118	17	0	2	0	0	0	1	1	1	0	0	1
R.Klesko dh-lf-1b	5	.100	10	2	1	0	0	0	1	2	4	0	0	1
B.Clontz p	3	.000	0	0	0	0	0	0	0	0	0	0	0	0
G.McMichael p	2	.000	0	0	0	0	0	0	0	0	0	0	0	0
G.Maddux p	1	.000	0	0	0	0	0	0	0	0	0	0	0	0
T.Wade p	2	.000	0	0	0	0	0	0	0	0	0	0	0	0
M.Wohlers p	3	.000	0	0	0	0	0	0	0	0	0	0	0	0
R.Belliard ss-dh	4	.000	0	0	0	0	0	0	0	0	0	0	0	0
S.Avery p	1	.000	0	0	0	0	0	0	0	0	0	0	0	0
M.Mordecai ph	1	.000	1	0	0	0	0	0	0	0	0	0	0	0
D.Neagle p	2	.000	1	0	0	0	0	0	0	0	1	0	0	0
E.Perez c	2	.000	1	0	0	0	0	0	0	0	0	0	0	0
M.Bielecki p	2	.000	1	0	0	0	0	0	0	0	1	0	0	0
T.Glavine p	1	.000	1	1	0	0	0	0	0	1	0	0	0	0
L.Polonia ph	6	.000	5	0	0	0	0	0	0	1	3	0	1	0
Totals	6	.254	201	26	51	9	1	4	26	23	36	3	4	4

NEW YORK	G	AVG.	AB	R	H	2B	3B	HR	RBI	BB	SO	SB	CS	E
K.Rogers p	1	1.000	1	0	1	0	0	0	0	0	0	0	0	0
L.Sojo ph-2b	5	.600	5	0	3	1	0	0	1	0	0	0	0	0
C.Fielder dh-1b	6	.391	23	1	9	2	0	0	2	2	2	0	0	0
J.Leyritz c-ph	4	.375	8	1	3	0	0	1	3	3	2	1	0	0
W.Boggs 3b-ph	4	.273	11	0	3	1	0	0	2	1	0	0	0	0
D.Jeter ss	6	.250	20	5	5	0	0	0	1	4	6	1	0	2
T.Raines lf	4	.214	14	2	3	0	0	0	0	2	1	0	1	1

	G	AVG.	AB	R	H	2B	3B	HR	RBI	BB	SO	SB	CS	E
J.Girardi c	4	.200	10	1	2	0	1	0	1	1	2	0	0	0
D.Strawberry lf-rf	5	.188	16	0	3	0	0	0	1	4	6	0	0	0
C.Hayes ph-3b-1b	5	.188	16	2	3	0	0	0	1	1	5	0	0	0
B.Williams cf	6	.167	24	3	4	0	0	1	4	3	6	1	0	0
P.O'Neill rf-ph	5	.167	12	1	2	2	0	0	0	3	2	0	0	0
T.Martinez 1b-ph	6	.091	11	0	1	0	0	0	0	2	5	0	0	0
M.Duncan 2b	6	.053	19	1	1	0	0	0	0	0	4	1	0	2
B.Boehringer p	2	.000	0	0	0	0	0	0	0	0	0	0	0	0
J.Key p	1	.000	0	0	0	0	0	0	0	0	0	0	0	0
G.Lloyd p	2	.000	0	0	0	0	0	0	0	0	0	0	0	0
J.Nelson p	3	.000	0	0	0	0	0	0	0	0	0	0	0	0
D.Weathers p	3	.000	0	0	0	0	0	0	0	0	0	0	0	0
J.Wetteland p	3	.000	0	0	0	0	0	0	0	0	0	0	0	0
A.Fox 2b-pr-dh-3b	4	.000	0	1	0	0	0	0	0	0	0	0	0	0
M.Aldrete rf-ph	2	.000	1	0	0	0	0	0	0	0	0	0	0	0
G.Lloyd p	1	.000	1	0	0	0	0	0	0	0	0	0	0	0
M.Rivera p	3	.000	1	0	0	0	0	0	0	0	0	0	0	0
D.Cone p	1	.000	2	0	0	0	0	0	0	0	1	0	0	0
A.Pettitte p	2	.000	4	0	0	0	0	0	0	0	1	0	0	0
Totals	6	.216	199	18	43	6	1	2	16	26	43	4	1	5

Atlanta	1 6 8	1 3 5	0 1 0	0 — 25
New York	1 0 3	2 1 3	0 6 0	2 — 18

DP: Atlanta 6, New York 7.
LOB: Atlanta 41, New York 48.
SAC: Atlanta, Lemke 2, Neagle, Dye.
New York, Jeter, Girardi.
SF: Atlanta, CJones, McGriff, Lopez.
New York, None.
GIDP: Atlanta, Lopez 2, Blauser, Lemke, McGriff, Jones, Pendleton.
New York, Boggs, Williams, Jeter, O'Neill.

ATLANTA	W-L	ERA	G	GS	CG	SV	IP	H	R	ER	BB	SO	HR
M.Bielecki	0-0	0.00	2	0	0	0	3.0	0	0	0	3	6	0
B.Clontz	0-0	0.00	3	0	0	0	1.2	1	0	0	1	2	0
T.Wade	0-0	0.00	2	0	0	0	0.2	0	0	0	1	0	0
J.Smoltz	1-1	0.64	2	2	0	0	14.0	6	2	1	8	14	0
T.Glavine	0-1	1.29	1	1	0	0	7.0	4	2	1	3	8	0

	W-L	ERA	G	GS	CG	SV	IP	H	R	ER	BB	SO	HR
G.Maddux	1-1	1.72	2	2	0	0	15.2	14	3	3	1	5	0
D.Neagle	0-0	3.00	2	1	0	0	6.0	5	3	2	4	3	0
M.Wohlers	0-0	6.24	4	0	0	0	4.1	7	3	3	2	4	1
S.Avery	0-1	13.50	1	0	0	0	0.2	1	2	1	3	0	0
G.McMichael	0-0	27.00	2	0	0	0	1.0	5	3	3	0	1	1
Totals	2-4	2.33	6	6	0	0	54.0	43	18	14	26	43	1

NEW YORK	W-L	ERA	G	GS	CG	SV	IP	H	R	ER	BB	SO	HR
J.Nelson	0-0	0.00	3	0	0	0	4.1	1	0	0	1	5	0
G.Lloyd	1-0	0.00	4	0	0	0	2.2	0	0	0	0	4	0
D.Cone	1-0	1.50	1	1	0	0	6.0	4	1	1	4	3	0
M.Rivera	0-0	1.59	4	0	0	0	5.2	4	1	1	3	4	0
J.Wetteland	0-0	2.08	5	0	0	4	4.1	4	1	1	1	6	0
D.Weathers	0-0	3.00	3	0	0	0	3.0	2	1	1	3	3	0
J.Key	1-1	3.97	2	2	0	0	11.1	15	5	5	5	1	0
B.Boehringer	0-0	5.40	2	0	0	0	5.0	5	5	3	0	5	2
A.Pettitte	1-1	5.90	2	2	0	0	10.2	11	7	7	4	5	1
K.Rogers	0-0	22.50	1	1	0	0	2.0	5	5	5	2	0	1
Totals	4-2	3.93	6	6	0	4	55.0	51	26	24	23	36	4

WP: Atlanta, Wohlers.
    New York, None.
PB: Atlanta, None.
    New York, None.
IBB: off Atlanta, Clontz (Strawberry), Avery (Williams), Wohlers (Leyritz).
    off New York, Weathers (McGriff), Wetteland (Klesko).
HBP: by Atlanta, Maddux (Jeter)
    by New York, Key (AJones)
BK: Atlanta, None.
    New York, Weathers.

Times of Games: 3:02, 2:44, 3:22, 4:17, 2:54, 2:52.
Attendances: (3 games at New York; 169,080).
              (3 games at Atlanta; 155,605).
Umpires: Jim Evans, Terry Tata, Tim Welke,
        Steve Rippley, Larry Young, Gerry Davis.

ABOUT THE AUTHORS

JOHN HARPER is a baseball columnist for the New York *Daily News*. He coauthored *The Worst Team Money Could Buy*, a book about the rise and fall of the New York Mets in the 1980s and '90s. Harper lives in Whippany, New Jersey, with his wife, Liz, and sons, Matt and Chris.

BOB KLAPISCH has covered baseball in New York since 1983 for the *New York Post*, the New York *Daily News*, and most recently the Bergen (N.J.) *Record*. His work has appeared in *Sports Illustrated, The Sporting News*, and *Inside Sports*, and he frequently provides baseball commentary on *NewSport*, a cable TV show. Klapisch lives in New Jersey.